Malthouse Monographs on Africa

Editor: Dafe Otobo, DPhil (Oxford),
Professor, University of Lagos, Lagos, Nigeria

Advisory Editorial Board

Malthouse Monographs on Africa

Malthouse Monographs on Africa are peer-reviewed works on Africa covering the six main areas of a) social sciences and development studies; b) history, law and international relations; c) environmental and agricultural studies; d) gender, refugee and conflict studies; e) strategic and defence studies; and f) labour and trades unions.

The Monographs are intended to provide an arena for free contestation of ideas and as outlet for research and empirical studies on Africa in the areas indicated above. The monographs thus have no links with, nor funded by, any African government or political party. Nor do the views expressed in them represent those of the editorial board.

Works for consideration may be of purely theoretical, or historical or applied in nature or policy-oriented. Such may be sent directly to the Editor as electronic files (dafeotobo2002@yahoo.co.uk) in Microsoft Word Rich Text format, or to the publishers (malthouse_press@yahoo.com}. Diskettes and hard copies may also be sent to the publishers at the address on the imprint page. The aim is to publish accepted works within three months.

Malthouse Monographs on Africa
Volumes 1 - 9

Guest Series Editor: Dayo Oluyemi-Kusa,
Director, External Conflict Prevention & Resolution,
Institute for Peace and Conflict Resolution, The Presidency,
Abuja, Nigeria

- Rotimi T. Suberu, *Institutional structure and process of government in Nigeria, 1985-1993*
- R. A. Akindele, *Federalism under General Babangida's administration in Nigeria*
- Dele Olowu & Kunle Awotokun, *Local government and the IBB administration*
- Cyril Obi, *The Nigerian private sector under adjustment and crisis 1985-1993*
- Bola A. Akinterinwa, *General Ibrahim Babangida's legacy: the domestic and international dimensions*
- Nereus I. Nwosu, *Nigeria's foreign policy under General Babangida*
- Antonia T. Oko-Osi, *Corruption and corrupt practices: institutionalization and legitimation under the Babangida Administration*
- Oyeleye Oyediran & Babafemi Badejo, *The military and democracy in Nigeria: the Political Bureau Report*
- Adekunle Amuwo, *Politics of the annulment of June 12 presidential election in Nigeria*

Malthouse Press Limited
43 Onitana Street, Off Stadium Hotel Road,
Surulere, Lagos, Nigeria
E-mail: malthouse_press@yahoo.com
malthouse_lagos@yahoo.co.uk
Tel: +234 (01) -773 53 44; 0802 364 2402

© Malthouse Monographs on Africa 2007
First Published 2007
ISBN 978 023 234 6

Distributors:
African Books Collective Ltd
Email: abc@africanbookscollective.com
Website: http://www.africanbookscollective.com

Guest Editor's comment

All the Monographs in this series attempt to explore and document events, policies and impact of the General Ibrahim Babangida-led military regime in Nigeria, covering the period 1985 to 1993. These contributions were originally for a book edited by me on that regime but other considerations, especially that of comprehensiveness of coverage of arguably the most momentous phase in Nigeria's post-Civil War socio-political development, led to the shelving of that idea. It was thought that a more useful scope or coverage might be achieved through a continuing development of Monographs on different facets of Nigerian society under this regime – a feat which may only be possible in a book so voluminous and whose cost might be such as to be out of the reach of the intended audience.

I should like to thank all the contributors who have waited this long to see their work in print, a fate that is unlikely to befall the contributors of the other titles currently in preparation. I am grateful to the publishers for including these titles in Malthouse Monographs for Africa family.

Dayo Oluyemi-Kusa

The Nigerian private sector under adjustment and crisis 1985-1993

Cyril Obi, PhD

Programme Coordinator, Post-Conflict Transition, the State and Civil Society in Africa, at the Nordic Africa Institute, Uppsala, Sweden, and an Associate Research Professor, the Nigerian Institute of International Affairs, Victoria Island, Lagos, Nigeria

No. 4

Contents

Introduction

The Babangida years (1985-1993) were a period of adjustment and crisis for the traumatized Nigerian economy. Between August 1985 when Babangida seized power in a palace coup and August 1993 when he 'stepped aside' as the head of state, there was a major shift in economic policy from state-led intervention to reliance on the market-mechanism to manage and resolve Nigeria's economic and debt crisis. This shift was the outcome of the following factors: increasing pressures from the International Monetary Fund, the World Bank and the creditor clubs, the desire of the Babangida regime to break the deadlock in talks with the IMF and World Bank, following the rejection of their "conditionalities" by its predecessors in office (Olukoshi, 1991:24-47), the global trend towards monetarist solutions to economic crises, and the desire to open blocked credit lines and restore confidence in the Nigerian economy, especially in the eyes of foreign investors and the donor community.

Before the Babangida junta seized power in 1985, Nigeria had been in the throes of a deep-seated national crisis, first noticed during the 1977-78 and 1981 oil shocks, when global oil prices, suddenly collapsed (Olukoshi, 1991). This crisis was thus linked to the refraction of the global capitalist crisis locally, and contradictions embedded within the Nigerian economy (Olukoshi, 1991). The collapse of global oil prices adversely affected Nigeria's extroverted oil-based economy. Specifically, it meant a sudden contraction in the supply of foreign exchange to run the import-dependent industries and foot the huge food import bill. It also meant a significant reduction in oil revenues accruing to the Nigerian state, raising questions about its legitimacy and capacity to pursue its brand of patrimonial capitalism. In an early effort to arrest the slide into further crisis, the Shagari administration promulgated the Economic Stabilization Act in 1982 (Olukoshi: 1991). The Act was directed at curtailing state expenditure and rationalizing imports. Shagari's mishandling of the economic crisis and the 1983 General Elections provided the military with the excuse to seize power in December 1983, through a coup that brought the Buhari-Idiagbon junta to power. The junta tried to arrest the crisis through an austerity programme which placed emphasis on local sourcing of raw materials, counter-trade of oil for essential imports, rejection of IMF-World Bank "conditionalities" such as the devaluation of the naira and the removal of petroleum subsidies, and the commitment of a substantial part of its external earnings to debt servicing. These efforts however did not elicit any real turnaround in the sharply declining economic fortunes, while the regime's authoritarianism alienated wide sections of the populace. This prepared the ground for the 1985 coup that brought Babangida to power.

On getting to power, one of the priorities of the Babangida administration was to reach an agreement with the IMF and World Bank. After a nationwide debate in which Nigerians rejected an IMF loan on the basis of its harsh conditionalities, the government in 1986 turned round to impose the structural adjustment programme (SAP) on Nigerians, under the guise that it was a 'home-grown' solution to the nation's crisis (Soremekun and Obi, 1994). With time it became clear that SAP was in reality an IMF and World Bank approved project wrapped in a nationalist garb, but, more fundamentally, based on a market-determined perspective of the Nigerian crisis. It had all the hallmarks of the monetarist-inspired standard IMF and World Bank prescriptions for all ailing Third World economies:

> At the heart of the market-based approach to the management of the national economic crisis which the Babangida regime adopted in 1986 was the devaluation of the naira, the deregulation of prices and interest rates, the privatization of public enterprises, the liberalization of trade the introduction of user prices and cost recovery measures, and the withdrawal of subsidies on petroleum products and fertilizer, among others (Olukoshi and Obi, 1994).

This shift from the 'state' to the 'market' through the deregulation of the Nigerian economy placed a lot of emphasis on the centrality of market forces in the efficient allocation of, and management of resources. It also placed a high premium on the revolutionary potential of the private sector, unfettered by an "inefficient, bloated and rent-seeking state" to act as a catalyst of economic recovery and growth. The logic of economic policy during the Babangida years was thus hinged on 'the rolling back of the state' from the economy, and covering its retreating tracks with those of private capital, under the hegemony of market forces.

The critical issue therefore is how Nigeria at the onset of the Babangida years arrived at "a historic turning point in the development of Nigerian capitalism" (Olukoshi, 1993). Closely related to this was the major role assigned to the private sector as the impetus of growth and recovery. These issues had implications for Nigeria's political economy, class relations and the role of the Nigerian state in the accumulation process; as well as the fortunes of the private sector itself. In the discussions that follow, the main issue is to examine if the private sector during the Babangida years was able to live up to the optimistic expectations of the authors of SAP and the market-based approach to economic crisis management. If it did not, what went wrong?

In seeking to address the foregoing issues, this monograph has been divided into five parts: the introduction, the historical background, the conceptual and theoretical issues, economic growth and contradictions, and the conclusion. At the end, it would be argued, that the private sector, like the public sector during the years 1985 to 1993, failed to bring about any meaningful transformation of the Nigerian economy. Structural adjustment and the market forces became a part of the Nigerian crisis, pushing further into the future, prospects of economic recovery and growth.

The historical background

The role of the private sector in the Nigerian economy is largely the product of its history, and Nigeria's objective position in the global economy. The term 'private sector' in this context refers to private capital or economic enterprises in which private and corporate shareholders own a greater bloc proportion of equity participation. Historically, there has been a symbiotic relationship between state and private capital, especially in states where private capital appeared weak or faced stiffer competition from stronger economies. Thus, our definition of the private sector takes this reality into consideration in its operationalization. It is also important to note that the private sector can be divided into the formal and the informal. Again this division is blurred in certain areas where strategies of multiple livelihoods and state patronage predominate. In this study, discussions of the private sector will be largely restricted to the organized private sector:

> ...the organized private sector approximates the modern economy of developed countries with their registered companies, trade and professional associations, banks, insurance and the paraphernalia of modern commerce (Eleazu, 1988:241).

Thus, attention will be focused on publicly quoted companies, trading and financial institutions, and the service companies as organized sectorally, or under groups such as the Manufacturers Association of Nigeria (MAN), and the National Association of Chambers of Commerce, Industry, Mines and Agriculture (NACCIMA), and the labour unions.

As noted earlier, the role of the private sector in the economy was largely influenced by its colonial origins, and its relationship with state capital within the ambience of the mixed economy framework. The Nigerian private sector emerged from the process of the forcible integration of Nigeria into the global capitalist system at the beginning of this century. The pre-capitalist formations that existed in what later became Nigeria were transformed into exporters of cheap primary products (agricultural cash crops, such as cotton, ground nuts and cocoa, and minerals such as tin, columbite, coal, and much later, petroleum) and a net importer of finished goods from the industries of the

Metropole. The colonial economy was thus designed to serve the needs of the global market and the colonializing power, Britain, and was divorced from its immediate domestic context (Obi, 1995). It was in this context of extraversion and exploitation that the private sector emerged. Its ethos was based on the exploitation of the vast Nigerian market by a few large highly integrated foreign merchant firms: United African Company (UAC), (British); John Holt (British); Peterson Zochonis (PZ), (British); Companie Francaise De L'Afrique Occidentale (CFAO), (French); Societe Commerciale de L'Afrique Occidentale (SCOA), (French), and the Union Trading Company (UTC), (Swiss) (Aju, 1994:124). They were soon joined by some Indian, Greek and Levantine merchant firms. Notable among the Indian firms were K. Chellaram and Sons, J.T. Chanrai and Co, Bhojson, Indian Emporium and Inlaks (Aju: 1994). Thus the early stages of the Nigerian private sector manifested its domination by foreign trading companies that had a monopoly of the import-export trade and paid no interest in, nor encouraged local industrialization (Obi, 1995). Nigerian participation was thus curtailed and insignificant. Although the colonial Nigerian economy expanded in terms of the growth in imports and exports, it did not undergo any real transformation as the commercial interests that dominated the private sector paid no attention to industrialization thrust was impelled by the growing strength of the decolonization movement and its economic nationalism, which necessitated a shift in the attitude of the companies towards industrialization. Part of the nationalist ideology of the independence movement, was rapid economic development centred on a strategy of import-substitution industrialization. This was significant in several respects:

the Nigerian state saw the pursuit of economic development as an important part of the independence project; the emergent Nigerian elite saw an opportunity in capturing the cash crop economic base of each of the country's three to accumulate surplus for class formation and reproduction. Central to this was the adoption of a strategy of state-led (capitalist) development. This use of the state, and political power to constitute or to transform themselves from a middle class into capitalist class took place in the context of Nigeria's further integration into the global capitalist system, and the sharing of the surplus from peasant-based agriculture. This partly explains each faction of the (regionalised) power elite worked hard to exclude the other from its regional base, and also did everything possible to crush the opposition. It also explains why the government adopted a mixed economy strategy on national development-based on an import-substitution strategy of development (ISI), which emphasized state interventionist and welfare roles, but also ensured that Nigeria's position in the international division of labour as an exporter of raw materials and importer of (semi) finished goods was preserved and reinforced. The assumption was that the development of the regional economic bases and the regionalist bourgeoisie would somehow lead to a tricking down of some of the benefits to the other groups in society.

However, the collapse in the global prices of cash crops in the mid-1960s created a new problem for the regional elite, more so, as attention had begun to shift to the growing importance of petroleum, which was found in the ethnic minority Niger Delta of the Midwestern and Eastern regions. According to Rimmer (1978: 149), while agricultural exports declined by 40 per cent between 1964 and 1974, the volume of oil exports increased five-fold during the same period. This rising significance of oil eventually contributed to a new struggle for the control of the Niger Delta. It basically led to a struggle between those that felt the oil should belong to the regions, and those that wanted it to belong to the federal government (Pearson 1970). While the former presented a problem to the ethnic minorities of the Niger Delta who felt that they had been marginalised for too long by the Igbo elite of the Eastern region, and preferred their own state/region outside as a guarantee of their local autonomy and control of the oil, the Eastern region and the federal government were both interested in controlling the oil.

Oil, was therefore one of the factors that led to the outbreak of the Nigerian civil war in 1967. This was after an abortive attempt by some Ijaw ethnic minority activists led by Isaac Adaka Boro to secede from Nigeria in February 1966 to a way of asserting their ownership of the oil under their lands and preventing the perceived attempt of the Eastern Region to seize "their" oil (in the Niger Delta). The three way struggle for the control of oil at the local, regional and national levels featured prominently in the war, when a faction of the local formed an alliance with the national elite to defeat Eastern secession and claims to the oil in the Niger Delta. The ethnic minorities of the Niger Delta did get their own states, but the effective control of the oil in the region shifted to the federal military government, which enacted series of decrees vesting the ownership of oil found in the Niger Delta, as well as the distribution of oil revenues in itself. Thus by the time the Nigerian civil war ended in 1970, a new centralist oil-based accumulation logic had replaced the regionalist cash-crop based one as the modality of Nigeria's class formation and integration into global capitalism. The new wealth from oil was seen as an asset for the construction of a post-civil war national unity project hinged upon a strong central/federal government and weak states. At the same time the new military rulers of Nigeria and their civilian advisers say oil as the strategic asset that would ensure a new nationalism based on oil-buoyed-development in which an indigenous capitalist class would emerge to play a more prominent role.

Thus, Nigeria's joining of the Organisation of Oil Exporting Countries (OPEC) in July 1971 was both an act of the new-found economic nationalism of the post-Civil War years, and the determination of the military rulers to tap into, and maximize the gains from the international politics of oil, which was beginning to tilt in favour of the OPEC countries. Within a few years, just as Nigeria's oil exports grew, international oil prices quadrupled an all oil OPEC member states, including Nigeria, experienced an oil windfall that was unprecedented in history. This windfall had far reaching consequences for class relations in Nigeria as well as the country's position in the international political economy.

For the Nigerian ruling class, the oil-boom presented an opportunity to re-negotiate the relationship between local and foreign capital, in favour of greater Nigerian participation in the commanding heights of the economy. The Nigerian state directed its attention at indigenous ownership/participation and control of strategic enterprises, and encouraged Nigerians to take up equity participation in the private sector. Through the Nigerian Enterprises Promotion Decrees of 1972 and 1977, the government sought to reserve certain economic activities for Nigerians, while insisting that the manufacturing sector reflected a majority Nigerian ownership structure (Ake, 1985: 173-

200). The thinking was that Nigerian ownership would shape the decisions and practices of these enterprises in favour of national development. Other expected benefits from this form of economic nationalism were, Nigerianization of management positions, transfer of technology and skills, employment and economic development. The attempt at the indigenization of the Nigerian economy was thus state-led, and took the form of a pronounced state capitalism, albeit side by side with private enterprise. This was the Keynesian golden age in Nigeria's political economy; an age in which oil was the fiscal basis of the state:

> Since the early 1970s oil has become the mainstay of the Nigerian economy. As a result of the quadrupling in oil price in 1973/74, Nigeria's oil revenue increased from less than ₦4.2 billion in 1974. By 1976, Nigeria's oil revenue had reached ₦6.3 billion and was at its peak in 1980 when oil revenue stood at about ₦12 billion (cited in Soremekun and Obi, 1994).

The sudden fall in global oil prices in 1981 led to a rapid drop in government revenues. By 1982, revenues had fallen to below half of the 1980 figures. Thus, the Nigerian state in the face of dwindling foreign exchange earnings could not meet up with the demands of the import-substitution industries. This forced the latter to take measures at saving costs. At the same time, the import bill outstripped export earnings, leading to a balance of payments crisis. The private sector was particularly hard-hit. Without foreign exchange to import raw materials and technology, most industries were shut down and thousands of workers were retrenched. State capitalism itself was in crisis. Faced with a shrinking fiscal base, the state found it difficult to foot the huge food import bill, prevent institutional decay, and even pay salaries of civil servants (Soremekun and Obi, 1994). The impact of the crisis was particularly devastating if one recalls, that the state's huge expenditure during the oil-boom years did not lead to any structural development of the economy, neither did it promote the integration of the oil sector with agriculture, or the industrial sectors of the Nigerian economy. Thus, the increased profile of state intervention in the foreign dominated private sector in the oil-boom years did not alter the structural weakness associated with the import-dependent ISI mode of industrialization within a restricted domestic market and based on a narrow range of consumer/light goods. Worse still, was the fact that the oil industry evolved as an enclave industry - without linkages with the domestic economy, being directly integrated with the global oil markets.

It can be argued, that expanded state intervention under the rubric of indigenization was more apparent than real. In fact, it signified an accommodation between state and private capital (Ake, 1985). As Ake correctly notes, the mere transfer of shares to Nigerians did not lead to the transfer of control, which continued to reside in the home countries of the multinationals that dominated Nigeria's private sector. This was in spite of the policy of Nigerianization of management positions in the private sector in which Nigerians were appointed to top 'honorific' positions (Edogun, 1985). In addition, many retired public officials, especially retired generals were appointed to the boards of banks and companies. This showed the unbiblical relationship between the state and the private sector, and how they served to reinforce, and protect their common interest in capitalist accumulation. Thus, the pattern of state expenditure favoured the private sector, even, if it was riddled with corruption. It has been pointed out for instance, that the indiscriminate importation of goods was under girded by foreign exchange fraud, leading to a situation in which Nigeria actually got 25 per cent of the real value of its imports (Olashore, cited in Bangura *et al.*; 1984: 12-16). Other forms of fraud included inflated contracts, various forms of 'white elephant' projects, transfer pricing and capital flight. All these, combined to exacerbate the structural weaknesses in the Nigerian economy.

When the second 'oil shock' struck in 1981, there was nothing to stop the Nigerian economic and external debt crisis. Government revenues from oil fell from ₦201 million in 1980 to ₦74.4 million 1981 and ₦55.8 million in 1982. In a context where the import bill rose from ₦0.098 billion in 1980 to ₦13.159 billion in 1981, the country fell into a balance of payments crisis, while the budget deficit began to grow. Despite the Shagari administration's 1982 Economic Stabilization Act, the crisis continued to deepen. Nigeria's Gross Product (GDP) fell by 5.9 % in 1981, 3.4 per cent in 1982 and 4.4 per cent in 1983 (CBN Report, 1981-84). The shortfall in foreign exchange earnings led to the virtual collapse of the private sector. The import-dependent industries without foreign exchange to import technology, spare parts and raw materials simply retrenched their workers and folded up (Olukoshi, 1993). According to a Manufacturers Association of Nigerian (MAN) survey, by July 1983, a total of 121 companies were shut down in the preceding twelve months (Olukoshi, 1991: 32). Also, between 1980 and 1983, an estimated one million workers lost their jobs. Even government-owned companies were similarly affected, while many state governments owed their workers up to six months' backlog of salaries (Olukoshi, 1991). The social misery index shot up in the face of massive retrenchment, unpaid salaries, high levels of unemployment and inflation and the collapse of social infrastructure and educational institutions. It was against this background of economic and social crisis, that the Shagari administration approached the International Monetary Fund (IMF) for an extended Fund facility of between ₦1.9 and ₦2.4 billion (Yahaya, 1993). In its response, the IMF gave a number of 'conditionalities' to qualify Nigeria for the facility: reduced government spending, privatization and commercialization of parastatals, rationalization of tariff structures, trade liberalization, introduction of sales taxes, an increased share for the private sector in credit issues, the phasing out of subsidies and quantitative import restrictions, and a reduction in budget deficits as well as a more widespread use of efficiency criteria for determining projects (Yahaya, 1993). The Shagari administration found these conditionalities unacceptable especially in an election year (Soremekun and Obi, 1994) leading to a lack of agreement with the IMF. It however, set up a presidential commission on parastatals in 1983, to investigate inefficiencies in the state sector. Unable to manage the economic crisis and a disputed electoral victory, the Shagari administration was overthrown on December 31, 1993, in a military coup that brought the Buhari-Idiagbon junta to power. Its strategy of managing the economic crisis was broadly based on maximizing oil earnings and minimizing the consumption of foreign exchange. Its discussions with the IMF ran into a deadlock when the junta rejected the IMF's conditionalities, particularly the removal of petroleum subsidies, the devaluation of the naira, the privatization of parastatals and public enterprises, and trade liberalization (Soremekun and Obi, 1994). In place of implementing these conditionalities, the regime resorted to counter-trade as a strategy of getting around the squeeze put on Nigeria by its creditors, circumvent the OPEC quota and reduce the foreign exchange dealings of the country. The government also encouraged industries to look for local alternatives to imported raw materials; while devoting 44 per cent of its foreign exchange earnings to debt servicing (Olukoshi, 1991). In a bid to explore ways of enhancing the efficiency of the state sector, the government set up a "Study Group on Statutory Corporations and State-Owned Enterprises and Public Utilities" in August 1984 to examine the causes of inefficiency of state-owned enterprises (SOEs), the desirability and methodology of privatization, possible methods for reviewing the management structure of the enterprises and ways in which cost recovery measures could be realized" (cited in Yahaya, 1993). The Study Group was largely in support of the privatization of parastatals provided this did not extend to areas that could be injurious to the "national interest" (Yahaya, 1993). The government in its response, rejected privatization and showed preference for commercialization. Economic nationalism, statism and authoritarianism did not resolve the crisis, thus it seemed natural that the junta would loose out, politically, when it was overthrown in another military coup in August 1985. That coup brought General Ibrahim Babangida to power.

From the foregoing, it is clear that the private sector in Nigeria was structurally ill-equipped to contribute to economic development. It is also obvious that although state participation in the economy became significant in the oil boom years, it did so in a manner that did not compete against or conflict with the private sector (Ake, 1985). In the face of the oil shocks, both public and private sectors were affected, but as the thinking in the mid-1980s suggested, state capitalism had failed. The option the historical moment then offered was that of private enterprise. It fell upon Babangida's lot to roll back the state and give free reign to the rule of market forces in a bid to manage and halt the march of the Nigerian crisis. The effort was conceived and implemented within the rubric of the structural adjustment programme.

Structural adjustment and the Nigerian private sector: some theoretical and conceptual considerations

Structural adjustment was conceptually committed to the reduction of the size of the state or public sector vis-à-vis the private sector. This rested on the assumption that market forces were most efficient for the rational allocation of resources. The logic dictated a shift from 'inefficient and corrupt' state intervention, to the efficient market mechanism. The shift from state initiative to the market mechanism was the outcome of the recession in global capitalism in the mid to late 1970s, and the replacement of the Keynesian 'mixed' economy model with the monetarist 'market' economy model. Other factors also influenced the shift. According to Yahaya, these included the perceived success of the Newly Industrialized Countries (NICs) amidst a deepening economic crisis in the Less Developed Countries (LDCs) which apparently placed greater reliance on the state rather than on the market; the ascent to power of conservative regimes in the key western industrialized countries, a development which encouraged the flourishing of right wing economic doctrines, and deep and extensive macro-economic and social crisis facing LDCs (Ake, 1985: 16).

Thus, import-substitution industrialization and public ownership were identified as causes of distortions, slow or negative growth, and the multiplication of inefficient structures (Ake, 1985). Before we proceed to examine linkages between SAP and the Nigerian private sector, it would be apposite to look at the recent ideological shift in neoclassical economics from Keynesianism to monetarism and its significance for contemporary developments in economic thinking a the global level.

Capitalism at the global level has been susceptible to periodic cycles of recession, linked to the crisis of accumulation. In the 1930s, the world was in the midst of an economic recession called the Great Depression. In a bid to break these cycles, John Keynes did a study in which he focused on the contradiction between savings and investment (Olukoshi, 1994:11-27). He concluded that unbridled market forces (laissez faire) could not alone achieve a correct balance between savings and investment, and that what was needed, was an interventionist state which would effectively maintain the balance, and solve the problem of market failure (cited in Olukoshi, 1994). Thus, Keynes' 'mixed' economy approach combined elements of laissez faire with and the regulatory and welfare roles of the state. It was a reprieve from the ruinous effects of the depression of the 1930s. Although Keynesianism contributed to recovery and growth in the West, it was unable to resolve the inflationary aspect of the crisis. Thus, by the 1970s when the global capitalist system fell again into recession, Keynesianism was clearly in decline. The monetarists led the paradigmatic shift directed at fighting the inflationary aspect of capitalist crisis. Monetarism was firmly committed to reducing money supply as one of the instruments of fighting inflation, but more fundamentally, it sought a reduced role for the state. Thus, the agenda of monetarism was to reinstate the unbridled reign of market forces, the retrenchment of the state from economic matters - on the basis of its inefficient interventionism (Olukoshi, 1994). It also included, the withdrawal of subsidies (as a means of cutting down inflationary public expenditure), elimination of subventions to public enterprises, devaluation, the privatization of enterprises and the jettisoning of fixed exchange rates

Contradictions and crisis (1985-1993)

The result of Babangida's rapprochement with the IMF and the World Bank was the acceptance of the 'market-driven approach' to resolving Nigeria's economic crisis. As noted earlier, Babangida's approach was a radical departure from the state-led interventionism of his predecessors. His earliest port of call in his 'marketization' drive as enunciated in his 1986 budget speech, was the removal of 'subsidies' from the pricing of local petroleum products to the tune of 80 per cent, to stem smuggling, promote exports, and encourage domestic savings to the tune of an anticipated sum of ₦900 million to be spent on the rehabilitation of social infrastructure, and the agricultural sector (cited in Soremekun 1995). On June 27, 1986, Babangida announced the adoption of the structural adjustment programme as the only solution to Nigeria's economic crisis. The main objectives of SAP were:

i.   to restructure and diversity the productive base of the economy in order to reduce dependence on the oil sector and imports;
ii. to achieve fiscal and balance of payments viability over the period (July 1, 1986 to June 1988);
iii. to lay the basis for sustainable non-inflationary growth; and
iv. to lessen the dominance of unproductive investments in the public sector, improve the efficiency and intensify the growth of the private sector.

The main features of SAP also included the:

i.   adoption of a realistic exchange rate policy;
ii.   rationalization and restructuring of tariffs;
iii. strengthening of demand management policies;
iv.   adopting measure to stimulate domestic production and broaden the supply base of the economy;
v.   adoption of appropriate pricing policies;
vi.   commercialization and or privatization of government parastatals;
vii. deregulation of the economy through the reduction/elimination of complex administrative controls, with greater reliance on market forces; and

viii. increased trade and payments liberalization (cited in Phillips, 1988).

Nigeria's SAP, like SAPs elsewhere, aimed at a monetarist solution to the country's economic crisis. It sought to retrench state-led capitalism and replace it with market-driven capitalism led by a strengthened private sector and a capitalist class. In relation to global accumulation, the deregulation of the Nigerian economy was expected to promote cheaper exports (via devaluation) and rationalize imports. However, trade liberalization was expected to open up the Nigerian economy to increased foreign investments, and enhance increased competitiveness of Nigerian products in the world market. At the heart of this 'revolution' was not only the private sector: local and foreign, but also the smaller, more specialized state, unburdened of the temptations of 'rent-seeking activities', as the state, theoretically-speaking would be separated from the economic realm.

In examining the linkages between SAP and the private sector between 1985 and 1993, our background already reveals that the relationship was premised on the belief that the SAP would establish the environment within which the private sector would act as the catalyst of economic growth. In the next part of this section, we shall test the validity of this assumption firstly by looking at the privatization and commercialization programme, which intended to install the 'market ethic' on what had been the state sector, and oversee the transfer of state enterprises to the private sector. This shall be followed, by an assessment of Nigeria's economic performance in the Babangida years by focusing on economic trends, the performance of the manufacturing sector, and the oil industry.

Privatization and commercialization: from State to market

The programme of privatization and commercialization of state-owned enterprises in Nigeria rested on the belief that the economic crisis had brought out the inefficiencies and inadequacies of these public enterprises (Ayodele, 1988). It rested upon the principle of the transfer of ownership of economic enterprises from the state to the private sector. As an integral part of SAP, Ayodele, and Yahaya, note that privatization was justified on several grounds: abysmally low returns on government investments in parastatals, conflicting objectives of some parastatals, growing burden on state funds, diversion of resources, political interference, the assumed superiority of the private sector (performance-wise as a result of the profit motive) over the inefficient and corrupt public sector, and the recommendations of earlier panels to study the problems of parastatals. It was also expected that privatization and commercialization would cut waste, and bring in some revenue into state coffers.

According to Babangida:

> We accepted the programme in the firm belief that it is necessary for the success of our economic reform programmes so that limited government resources normally allocated to these institutions as subventions could be released for the implementation of other viable projects that would benefit the entire society (Keynote address, cited in Olagunju and Jinadu, 1991: 129).

He went further to justify the programme, which had by then yielded about ₦277,504,155.00 in revenue from the privatization of 18 out of 144 designed companies. Other advantages dangled by Babangida include the promotion of social equity through the distribution of shares, the promotion of greater efficiency, productivity and accountability, and the determination of his administration to leave behind a free enterprise economy.

Table 1: **Summary of Federal Government's investments up to November, 1990**

Sector	Equity Holding ₦	Local Loans ₦	Subvention ₦	Total Investment ₦
1. Agro-Allied/ Manufacturing Mining Company	2670236561	3694112650	1745545275	810894485
2. Financial Institutions:				
- Banks	1135649348	435496551	10361000	1581597900
- Insurance	180224568	-	-	180224568
3. Service:				
- NNPC	6398373000	-	599598000	6997972000
- Others	7182323192	6471735912	-	13654059290
4. External Investment	261323378	15072795	-	276415987
5. Invest-Forfeited to Federal Government	769868	-	-	794686
6. Loans to: Statutory Corp.	-	1312875312	3144817661	4457692923
Loans: without terms	-	910682615	294345615	1205028230
Total	**17829035734**	**12839975835**	**5795604525**	**36464616094**

Source: Ministry of Finance Incorporated (MOFI), Lagos, Nov. 1990

Through Decree No. 25 of 1988, Babangida provided a legal framework for the programme of privatization and commercialization of state enterprises. Decree 25, led to the establishment of the Technical Committee on Privatization and Commercialization (TCPC) to draw up, oversee and implement the programme of transition from 'state to market.' The TCPC swung into action, but it attempted to distinguish between privatization and commercialization. In the TCPC's view,

> Privatization is an umbrella term to describe a variety of policies, which encourage competition and emphasize the role of market forces in place of statutory restrictions and monopoly powers, (the Presidency, TCPC Final report, Vol. 1: 13).

While commercialization referred to:

> ...reorganization of enterprises wholly or partially owned by the government, in which such commercialized enterprises shall operate as profit-making commercial ventures without subvention from the government (TCPC) Report).

The main difference between privatization and commercialization lay in the ownership structure, while they were united by the profit motive and the rational use of resources. The TCPC in carrying out its task grouped public enterprises into five categories: Fully privatized, partly privatized, fully commercialized, partly commercialized, and state enterprises, which were too strategic to be either privatized or commercialized. While 111 enterprises were slated for full or partial privatization, another 34 were slated for full or partial commercialization (Ayodele, 1988). (See Tables 2 and 3 below)

Table 2: **Public Enterprises for Partial and Full Privatization**

Sector	No. of Companies	Type
Development Banks	4	Partial Privatization
Commercial & Merchant Banks	12	"
Oil Marketing Companies	3	"
Steel Rolling Mills	3	"
Air & Sea Travels	2	"
Motor Vehicle Assembly Plants	6	"
Paper Mills	3	"
Sugar Companies	3	"
Cement Companies	5	"
Hotels and Tourism	4	Full Privatization
Textile Companies	3	"
Transportation Companies	4	"
Food & Beverages Companies	6	"
Agric. & Livestock Production	18	"
Salt Companies	2	"
Wood & Furniture Companies	2	"
Insurance Companies	14	"
Film Production & Distribution	2	"
Flour Milling	1	"
Cattle Ranches	2	"
Construction & Engineering Coy.	4	"
Dairy Companies	2	"
Others	4	"
Total Number of Affected Enterprises	111	"

Source: TCPC Final Report Vol. 1 (Main Report)

Table 3: **Public Enterprises for partial and Full Commercialization**

Enterprises	No. of Companies	Type
River Basin Dev. Authorities	11	Partial Commercialization
Nigerian Railway Corp.	1	"
Nigerian Airport Authority	1	"
N.E.P.A.	1	"
Nig. Sec. Ptg. Minting Ltd.	1	"
National Provident Fund	1	"
Delta Steel Company Ltd.	1	"
Ajaokuta Steel Co. Ltd.	1	"
Nig. Machine Tools Ltd.	1	"
Federal Housing authority	1	"
Kainji Lake National Park	1	"
Federal Radio Corporation	1	"
Nig. TV Authority	1	"
News Agency of Nigeria	1	"
Nig. National Pet. Corp.	1	Full Commercialization
Nigeria Telecom (NITEL) Ltd.	1	"
Associated Ores Mining co.	1	"
Nigerian Coal Corporation	1	"
Nat. Ins. Corp. of Nigeria	1	"
Nigeria Re-Insurance Corp.	1	"
National Properties Ltd.	1	"
T.B. Square Mgt. Committee	1	"
Nigerian Ports Authority	1	"
Total Number of Enterprises to be Commercialized	34	"

Source: TCPC Final Report Vol. 1 (Main Report)

According to TCPC claims, within four years it was able to privatize 88 out of the 111 enterprises slated for full or partial privatization (TCPC report). It "offered some 1,486,772,063 shares to Nigerians from all walks of life and in the process raised ₦3.3 billion as revenue for government." The TCPC in the same breath, signed Performance Agreements with 26, out of the 30 parastatals slated for commercialization.

The performance of the private sector under SAP

The performance of the private sector under the Babangida years (which roughly corresponded with the SAP years) is best captured against the background of the performance of the economy in general. As mentioned earlier, the aim of economic policies were, to curb inflation, encourage domestic savings and investments, and the exports of non-oil goods, especially manufactures (Olukoshi and Obi, 1995). The policy instruments ranged from financial and monetary reforms, tariff reforms, sectoral credit guidelines, deregulation of the foreign exchange market, the sale of state shares in public enterprises an the liberalization of the external trade and payments systems. In spite of all these the 'Babangida miracle' premised on economic liberalization never came to be; rather, it compounded the Nigerian economic crisis:

> As it turned out, the attempt at economic liberalization was to complicate the national economic crisis even more. In spite of the massive and repeated devaluation of the naira, with the currency falling on the official market from a position of near parity to the American dollar at the

beginning of the adjustment process in 1986 to nearly 22 to the dollar at the end of 1993 (the parallel market rate ranged between 40-50 naira to the dollar at the end of 1993), and the deregulation of interest rates which saw interest rates rising as high as 45% (at one point they hovered around 60%), the adjustment programme failed to make a significant impact on the economy and lives of ordinary Nigerians (Olukoshi and Obi, 1995).

The inflationary spiral coupled with the fiscal indiscipline of the military junta totally eroded the quality of life of Nigerians. With the oil sector in crisis, the shift to, and the expected boom in the non-oil sector failed to materialize, with the state having no option but to depend on the export of crude oil.

Nigeria's major macro-economic indices offered very little succour between 1986 and 1993. Although official statistics continued to record modest GDP growth rate sat an average of 4 per cent, the breakdown revealed that very little growth occurred in the agricultural and industrial sectors:

The country's main macro economic indices were poor for much of the period 1986-1993. Not only was the budget never balanced, the national fiscal deficit ballooned almost on an annual basis. The national debt burden remained heavy and was a constant drain on the foreign exchange earnings accruing to the state. Non-oil export production, including the production of traditional agricultural exports, remained very sluggish, falling far short of all projections. Foreign investment flows to the economy were insignificant in spite of the embrace of a new, more liberal investment code and the

government's adoption of debt-equity conversion as
a strategy for managing the country's external debt
(Olukoshi and Obi, 1995).

The economic crisis led to the fall of the per capita
income of Nigerians from $1,000 1980 to $320 in 1992.
Thus Nigeria's ranking fell from that of a medium, to a
low-income country. Figures for budget deficits grew from
₦1.118 billion in 1985 to ₦13.69 billion in 1989 and
reaching a peak of ₦81 billion in 1994. Thus, the deficit as
a proportion of the GDP continued to rise and in 1993 it
rose to 12.3 %, according to official sources (*CBN Report*,
1993: p. 3).

On the external front, the economic profile offered no
respite. The current account deficit continued to widen in
the face of the poor performance of both the oil and non-oil
sectors (*CBN Report*, 1993: 127). According to CBN
sources,

...the current account was largely in deficit for
most of the period 1988-1993 except in 1990. It
further noted that as a proportion of GDP, the
current deficit was 2.0 per cent compared with an
average of 0.6 % between 1989 and 1992. The
poor current account position over the years
reflected the high levels of scheduled interest
payments, the general weakness in international oil
prices and expansionary fiscal policy.

The manufacturing sector

The failure of SAP to bring about positive economic
change, reflected largely in the real sectors of the economy,
particularly, manufacturing. High production costs,

depressed domestic demand, and the dumping of cheap and more competitive products in Nigerian markets hurt local manufacturing. The deregulation of interest rates and the massive devaluation of the naira made it very difficult for manufacturers to source credit, while tariff reforms in most cases opened the doors to more competitive imports. Even in cases where profits were declared, there were worth only a fraction of the published figures due to the high rate of inflation and the massive depreciation of the naira (*National Concord*, April 6, 1990: 3). The private sector did not only suffer from the poor state of the economy, its plight was further worsened by capital flight and disinvestment. Thus, some key foreign companies withdrew their investments from Nigeria, and they were not replaced. The list included: Barclays Bank, Bank of America, Chase Manhattan, First Chicago, British Leyland, Tate and Lyle, Sanyo, International Chemical Industries (ICI) and Boots (*National Concord*, ibid., 1990).

In its review of economic performance in 1993, the Manufacturers Association of Nigeria lamented SAP's failure:

> The persistent drag in industrial recovery...epitomizes the failure of the orthodox macro-economic policies of the Structural Adjustment Programme (SAP) to induce appropriate, positive response (*MAN Reviews*, 1990-93, and Duru in the *Nigeria Economist*, 1993: 12).

Thus, the private sector from 1986 continued to suffer from low levels of investment, sharp declines in profit margins in spite of apparent increases in sales turnover. Between 1990 and 1993 capacity utilization of the manufacturing sector fell from 37 per cent to 28.89%, with those sub-sectors that were most dependent on imported raw materials, being the most badly affected. Thus, sub-sectors such as basic metal, iron and steel, fabricated metal products, plastics and rubber, electrical and electronics, chemicals and pharmaceutical, motor vehicle and miscellaneous assembly fared poorly, recording the lowest capacity utilization percentages (*MAN reports*, 1990-93).

The crisis in money supply and credit offered the private sector very little succour. Money supply continued to grow largely due to government's fiscal irresponsibility, devaluation and the rapid expansion of the banking and non-banking financial sector. With inflation out of control, the free fall of the naira and high interest rates, the abnormal growth of the banking system blocked prospects of growth in manufacturing.

Thus, between 1986 and 1993, the industrial and manufacturing sectors of the private sector performed dismally, deepening Nigeria's economic crisis, against all the predictions of the ideologues of structural adjustment.

The petroleum sector

The petroleum sector was the earliest to receive the adjustment pill when 80 per cent of subsidies on the domestic prices of petroleum products were removed in one fell swoop (Soremekun and Obi, 1994). This was followed by the re-organization and commercialization of the NNPC in January 1988, while state-owned shares in oil marketing companies were sold to members of the public. Between 1985 and 1993, domestic prices of petroleum products were raised five times in a bid to narrow the gap between domestic and international prices, raise more revenue for government and rationalize local consumption of petroleum products, in order to free more for export and earn foreign exchange.

The Nigerian government under Babangida offered many 'sweeteners' to foreign oil companies to invest in the Nigerian oil sector. This took the form of Memoranda of Understanding which offered attractive terms to oil investors. In response, Shell, Statoil-BP, Exxon, Mobil, Agip (ENI) and ELF (now Total) made additional investments in new exploration blocks. Indigenous investors generally kept a low profile, or restricted themselves to small fields, or the marketing of refined products.

However, as I argued elsewhere, (Obi, 1994) the market reforms did not resolve the crisis of the Nigerian oil industry. The industry largely remained dependent on the fortunes of the global market, while on the domestic scene it operated with very little forward or backward linkages with other sectors in the economy. Although the NNPC was reorganized and commercialized, it continued to witness a great deal of state interference, in the latter's bid to raise more revenue for national needs, and for oiling the wheels of its patron-client networks. The NNPC thus suffered from frequent political interference and its relative weakness vis-à-vis the oil multinationals it was supposed to regulate and compete against. To worsen the situation, by 1993 the NNPC was owed the oil companies over $500 million, being its unpaid share of joint venture investments in the oil industry, a development, that clearly dampened the enthusiasm of the oil companies that were operating within the context of a depressed global market, increasing costs, and growing security threats arising from popular protests in the oil producing areas.

Thus, as in the case of the manufacturing sector, SAP in the oil industry did not fare better. Due to the monocultural character of the economy and the absence of growth in the real sector, the state was hard-pressed to resist its retrenchment from the lucrative oil sector. Thus, it dug in, in defiance of the market forces. The removal of subsidies rather than free more resources for development, fed into inflation, raised production costs for the manufacturing sector, fuelled state patrimonialism and made life worse for most Nigerians. Rather than contribute to economic development, the oil sector remained trapped in its technological dependence, subject to the vagaries of the global market and the exigencies of Nigeria's extraverted economy, and domestic politics.

Conclusion

From the foregoing, it is clear that the economic policies introduced by the Babangida junta between 1985 and 1993 turned out to be disastrous for the Nigerian private sector. Save for the providential oil sub-sector, which as we have shown suffered some decline, the dreams of a monetarist miracle became a nightmare. By 1993, the economic crisis was further compounded by the democratic struggles against authoritarianism, crippling nationwide strikes, the unceremonious exit of the Babangida junta and the unclear steps of the short-lived transition government, against the background of world opprobrium at the cancellation of Nigeria's 1993 presidential election by Babangida's military government. These developments contributed to another wave of capital flight, disinvestment, and scared off would-be investors, thus mortally wounding the already stressed private sector.

The years 1985 to 1993 were particularly bad for labour. Millions of workers were retrenched and lost their jobs as a result of the economic policies adopted by government. However, labour, along with other pro-democracy groups, were able to resist some unpopular economic policies, although at a heavy cost.

What comes out forcefully is that the state form in Nigeria in the Babangida years, domesticated structural adjustment to suit its own agenda of accumulation, by creating the conditions of its reproduction by manipulating state retrenchment into consolidation.

Thus, the opportunity offered by the historical moment for a Nigerian capitalist revolution was subverted. It showed more than any thing else, that the state-form, and character of the private sector were contradictory to any process of real economic growth or national development. More fundamentally, it exposed the inability of SAP to address and resolve Nigeria's economic crisis. Therefore, the prospects for growth in post-adjustment post-Babangida Nigeria lie in a radically different democratic/developmental state form and productive mode of accumulation centred on the coalition of social forces, which resolutely oppose SAP and authoritarianism.

References

Aju, A. (1994) *Industrialization and Technological Innovation in an African Economy*, Lagos: Regional Centre for Technology Management (RECTEM).

Ake, C. (1985) ed., *Political Economy of Nigeria, London:* Longmans.

Akeredolu-Ale, E. (1972) 'The Comparative Threshold. Hypothesis and Nigeria's Industrialization Process - A Review Article,' *Nigerian Journal of Economic and Social Studies*, Vol. 14, No. 1.

Ayodele, A. (1988) 'Privatization and Commercialisation of Public Enterprises and their Implications.' in, A. Phillips and E. Ndekwu (eds) *Economic Policy and Development in Nigeria*, Ibadan: NISER.

Central Bank of Nigeria (1993) *CBN Annual Report and Statements for the Year Ended 31st December*, Lagos: CBN.

Duru, D. (1993) 'The Threat of Extinction,' in *The Nigerian Economist*, March 15.

Edogun, C. (1985) 'The Structure of State Capitalism in the Nigerian Petroleum Industry,' in C. Ake (ed.) *Political Economy of Nigeria*, London: Longmans.

Eleazu, U (1988) (ed) *Nigeria: The First Twenty Five Years*, Lagos and Ibadan: Infodata and Heinemann.

National Concord (1990) April 6.

Manufacturers' Association of Nigeria (1990-93 *MAN Review*), Lagos: MAN.

Obi, C. (1995) 'The Oil Sector and Nigeria's Industrialization,' in A. Olukoshi *et al.*, *Industrialization in Nigeria: Problems and Prospects*, Tokyo: Institute of Developing Economies (IDE).

Obi, C. (2001) `The Changing Forms of Identity Politics in Nigeria under Economic Adjustment: The Case of the Oil Minorities Movement of the Niger Delta, *Research Report* no. 119, Uppsala: Nordiska Afrikainstitutet.

Oderinde, A. (1992) 'Ex-soldiers Take Lion Share,' *The Punch*, January 23.

Ohiorhenuan, J. (1987) 'Recolonizing Nigerian Industry: the first year of the Structural Adjustment Programme,' in A. Phillips and E. Ndekwu (eds) *Structural Adjustment in a Developing Economy*, Ibadan: NISER

Olagunju, T. and Jinadu, L. (1991) *For Their Tomorrow We Give our Today: Selected Speeches of IBB*, Vol. II, London and Ibadan: Safari Books (in Association with Spectrum Books) n.d.

Olashore, O. (1984) cited in Article, Y. Bangura, R. Mustapha and S. Adamu, 'The Deepening Economic Crisis and its Political Implications,' *Africa Development,* Vol. III, No. 3.

Olukoshi, A. (1991) (ed.) *Crisis and Adjustment in the Nigerian Economy*, Lagos: JAD Publishers.

Olukoshi, A (1993), The *Politics of Structural Adjustment in Nigeria*: London: James Currey.

Olukoshi, A and Obi, C. (1994) `The Nigerian Economy: Retrospect and Prospect', in Ibrahim, J. (ed) *Population, Space and Development in Nigeria*, Abidjan: OECD/ADB.

Olukoshi, A *et al.* (1994) (ed.) *Structural Adjustment in West Africa*, Lagos: NIIA and Pumark.

Pearson, S. (1970) *Petroleuum in the Nigeria Economy*, California: Stanford University Press.

Rimmer, D. (1978) 'Elements of Political Economy', in Panterbrick, S. (ed) *Soldiers and Oil: The Political Transformation of Nigeria,* London: Frank Cass.

Soremekun K. (ed.) (1995) *Perspectives on the Oil Industry,* Lagos: Amkra Publishers, 1995.

Soremekun K. and Obi, C. (1994) `The Structural Adjustment Programme and the Nigerian Oil Industry,' *Nigerian Journal of International Affairs*, No. 1, Vol. 20.

Technical Committee on Privatization and Commercialization (TCPC) *Final Report* Volume 1 (Main Report), 1989.

Yahaya, S. (1993) 'The Privatization Programme of the Nigerian State', in Olukoshi, A. (ed) *The Politics of Structural Adjustment in Nigeria*, London: James Currey.

Malthouse Monographs on Africa

Editor: Dafe Otobo, DPhil (Oxford),
Professor, University of Lagos, Lagos, Nigeria

Advisory Editorial Board

Malthouse Monographs on Africa

Malthouse Monographs on Africa, new on the scene, are peer-reviewed works on Africa covering the six main areas of a) social sciences and development studies; b) history, law and international relations; c) environmental and agricultural studies; d) gender, refugee and conflict studies; e) strategic and defence studies; and f) labour and trades unions.

The Monographs are intended to provide an arena for free contestation of ideas and as outlet for research and empirical studies on Africa in the areas indicated above. The monographs thus have no links with, nor funded by, any African government or political party. Nor do the views expressed in them represent those of the editorial board.

Works for consideration may be of purely theoretical, or historical or applied in nature or policy-oriented. Such may be sent directly to the Series Editor as electronic files (dafeotobo2002@yahoo.co.uk) in Microsoft Word Rich Text format, or to the publishers (malthouse_press@yahoo.com}. Diskettes and hardcopies may also be sent to the publishers at the address on the imprint page. The aim is to publish accepted works within three months.

Malthouse Monographs on Africa
Numbers 1 – 10

Guest Series Editor: Dayo Oluyemi-Kusa,
Director, External Conflict Prevention & Resolution, Institute for Peace and Conflict Resolution, The Presidency, Abuja, Nigeria

- Rotimi T. Suberu, *Institutional structure and process of government in Nigeria, 1985-1993*
- R. A. Akindele, *Federalism under General Babangida's administration in Nigeria*
- Dele Olowu & Kunle Awotokun, *Local government and the IBB administration*
- Cyril Obi, *The Nigerian private sector under adjustment and crisis 1985-1993*
- Bola A. Akinterinwa, *General Ibrahim Babangida's legacy: the domestic and international dimensions*
- Nereus I. Nwosu, *Nigeria's foreign policy under General Babangida*
- Antonia T. Oko-Osi, *Corruption and corrupt practices: institutionalization and legitimation under the Babangida Administration*
- Oyeleye Oyediran & Babafemi Badejo, *The military and democracy in Nigeria: the Political Bureau Report*
- Adekunle Amuwo, *Politics of the annulment of June 12 presidential election in Nigeria*

Malthouse Press Limited
43 Onitana Street, Off Stadium Hotel Road,
Surulere, Lagos, Lagos State
E-mail: malthouse_press@yahoo.com
malthouse_lagos@yahoo.co.uk
Tel: +234 (01) -773 53 44; 0802 364 2402

© Malthouse Monographs on Africa 2007
First Published 2007
ISBN 978 023 235 4

Distributors:
African Books Collective Ltd
Email: abc@africanbookscollective.com
Website: http://www.africanbookscollective.com

Guest Editor's comment

All the Monographs in this series attempt to explore and document events, policies and impact of the General Ibrahim Babangida-led military regime in Nigeria, covering the period 1985 to 1993. These contributions were originally for a book edited by me on that regime but other considerations, especially that of comprehensiveness of coverage of arguably the most momentous phase in Nigeria's post-Civil War socio-political development, led to the shelving of that idea. It was thought that a more useful scope or coverage might be achieved through a continuing development of Monographs on different facets of Nigerian society under this regime – a feat which may only be possible in a book so voluminous and whose cost might be such as to be out of the reach of the intended audience.

I should like to thank all the contributors who have waited this long to see their work in print, a fate that is unlikely to befall the contributors of the other titles currently in preparation. I am grateful to the publishers for including these titles in Malthouse Monographs for Africa family.

Dayo Oluyemi-Kusa

General Ibrahim Babangida's legacy:
domestic and international dimensions

Bola A. Akinterinwa, PhD

Research Associate Professor at the Nigerian Institute of International Affairs, Victoria Island, Lagos, Nigeria.

No. 5

Contents

Introduction

One great problem confronting Nigeria is that Nigerians do not know what the problem of Nigeria is. It is doubtful whether Nigerians even accept that Nigeria does not only have problems also constitutes the main problem. It is in defence of Nigeria that policy decisions are said to be taken by government. It is similarly in defence of the same Nigeria that opponents of the government do oppose government policies. The problem, however, is that what Nigeria's exact political problem is, what Nigeria should be, and how Nigerians should go about this has never been made clear. If it has, most Nigerians are yet to agree on it. What is clear is that Nigeria has, since her independence on 1 October 1960, been engaged, but unsuccessfully, in the search for a stable polity.

Suffice it to recall that the unresolved different political contradictions of the early 1960s led to the Biafran crisis. The first military intervention in politics in January 1966, which provoked the counter-coup of July 1967, became a reference points for future coup makers in Nigeria. In fact, coups d'etats have become fashionable in Nigeria, as long as they were successful. Generally, military coups against military governments in Nigeria have been informed more by personality clash than by alleged national questions (corruption, mismanagement, economic poverty, etc.) which allegedly informed military coups against civilian governments. Consequently, when military officers plan to take over power by force, with a declared intention to correct the social ills in the society, they often ended up, because of personality clash, in intra-military wranglings, and by so doing, focused on how to maintain military security and stability rather than focusing on correcting the social ills which civilians were initially found quality of.

By seeking military security and stability, little or no time was given societal ills. Additionally, in the process of trying to correct societal ills, the military only succeeded in compounding existing problems, the most serious of which seems to be their non-preparedness to readily hand over the instrument of power to civilian politicians.

Officers not only quickly reached the peak of their career but were also quickly retired, especially at a time the Nigerian people were expecting the returns of their investments on them.

It is under this type of circumstance that General Ibrahim Badamasi Babangida (IBB) came to power on 27 August 1985. Although, as noted earlier, one major reason for coup d'tats in Nigeria is personality clash, the rationale for the August 1985 coup, as explained by IBB, is General Buhari's policy of "retaliatory reaction" and the inability of the government to reverse the downward trend of the economy. Put differently, IBB contested the confrontational policy attitude of the Buhari government and believed that the economy ought to be revamped. He believed that he could actually revamp the economy. In between 1985 and 1993, when he was compelled to "step aside" IBB appeared to have done his best for Nigeria but there is nothing to suggest that his best was acceptable to Nigerians.

At the international level, IBB enjoyed a lot of goodwill and support when he first took over power. Nigeria's foreign policy can be described as successful under IBB. At the hoe level, the story is different. IBB, within a period of six years, took a number of decisive measures: introduction corps programme, new foreign policy posture, proliferation of financial and banking institutions, organisation of a 'Concert of Medium Powers', introduction of economic diplomacy, creation of new social institutions and states, etc. In fact, he introduced new dimensions to the Nigerian polity which created new burdens and which neither the succeeding governments nor the people can grapple with easily. More important, the legacy bequeathed by IBB to Nigerians as a parting gift has also constituted a major impediment to political transition in Nigeria and has eventually broken the cord of relationship between the international community and the Nigerian people. This situation raises the problem of reconciliation between good governance and protection of national interests.

In this monograph, attempt is made to identify and analyse IBB's legacy through his style of governance and policies and how this legacy has adversely affected political transition and, more significantly, Nigeria's foreign relations.

IBB's legacy

When IBB took over power, he had his own vision for Nigeria. He introduced a self-styled policy attitude which we here call 'babangidomania.' Unlike Major-General Buhari's confrontational posture, 'babangidomania' encouraged openness and compromise, particularly with the western financial powers. It encouraged Nigerians to be actively involved in the search for solutions to Nigeria's problems but without necessarily accepting their recommendations.

'Babangidomania' has philosophical and ideological contents and is designed to enable IBB to have his own imprint on and control over foreign and domestic policies. This, in fact, made his style of government quite distinct from that of the preceding seven heads of state.

First, babangidomania as a philosophy can be understood from the way IBB perceived the solutions to Nigeria's problems. He believed that for Nigeria's mountainous, political and socio-economic problems to be solved, some fundamental structures of the Nigerian society must first be altered. He also believed that the military government is not simply a care-taker and a corrective administration but one which should "purposefully engage the nation's body politic and seek to transform society."[1] Thus, General Babangida did not only have a vision of Nigeria but also wanted to transform it.

Babangidomania has three philosophical underpinnings: a) there was the need to present the Babangida administration as a regime with fresh, original ideas and having determination to break with tradition or with the so-called controversial, 'national character;' b) unrest and insecurity could be better managed by appointing more controllable young military officers as state administrators and by ensuring that the immediate subordinate of General Babangida had little or no power of decision-making; c) effective presidential control over government affairs and general public support were crucial to good governance. So he believed that most of the enlightened Nigerians should be involved in the search of solutions to major national

---

[1] *Africa Confidential*, vol. 29, no. 4, February 19, 1988, p.6.

problems. This partly explains why he introduced an "open-door policy" or "citizen participation" as put by IBB himself.

Secondly, as a style of government, 'babangidomania' is characterised by simplicity, surprises and unpredictability, like dribbling in a good game of football. General Babangida was described as Nigeria's 'Maradona.' It is not clear whether 'Maradona' is complimentary. While Maradona is an undisputed good football player of world ranking, he is also of a shoddy character: he had been sanctioned for indiscipline and abuse of drugs. Whatever the case, IBB rejected the idea of heavy escort and excessive protocol whenever he was officially moving from one place to the other. In most cases, he used a Peugeot 504 saloon car without disturbing public tranquillity with noisy siren. In fact, he avoided making speeches especially where expected.[2] Consequently, at the initial stage, his policy attitude appeared to significantly endear him to Nigerians and many western leaders. At the end of his rule, like all other Nigerian leaders who often started well but generally failed to know when to quit the stage when ovations were loudest, IBB succeeded in having more critics and opponents than sympathisers. The analysis of the domestic and international aspects of the legacy, both as a philosophy and style of governance, is relevant at this juncture. This will bring into sharper focus the elements of babangidomania and how it affected national life and Nigeria's foreign relations.

---

[2] See, for instance, *National Concord*, June 21, 1990, pp. 1 and 2.

The domestic content

Building a new Nigeria: Babangidomania and the transformation of society

First, as noted earlier, 'babangidomania' is a set of new, original ideas aimed at breaking up with the tradition and transforming the society. In this context, General Babangida tried to dissociate himself from the image and records of his two predecessors by making changes in the official nomenclature. General Babangida changed his designation as "head of state" to that of a "president" and was referring to his government as 'Babangida administration,' thus giving the impression of an elected government. He changed the designation of the 'Supreme Military Council,' which was the highest decision-making authority, to 'Armed Forces Ruling Council (AFRC). This new designation took effect from August 30, 1985. The 'Supreme Headquarters' was renamed 'General Headquarters' and headed by a Chief of General Staff (CGS). The CGS was mainly concerned with non-military assignments and had "no special decision-making power", unlike under Major-General Muhammed Buhari when the CGS "had enormous power." General Babangida, by so doing, "has thus arranged matters so that he and a handful of close friends will control policy."[3]

In 1988, he restructured the civil service to his own advantage in order to broaden presidential control over

---

[3] *Africa Confidential*, vol. 26, no. 18, September 4, 1985. p. 1.

government affairs, particularly in the economic areas. In his 1988 budget speech, for instance, he announced that ministers would henceforth be both "chief executive" and "accounting officers" of their ministries. He therefore changed the designation of 'permanent secretary' to 'director-general' who was required to retire with the government that appointed him or her, and unless he or she was re-appointed by succeeding administrations. Thus, the character of 'permanentness' of the secretaries was removed as directors-general were henceforth considered as "political appointees".

He also made it clear that each ministry would be professionalised, that every office would also henceforth make his career entirely in the ministry or department of his choice, and that each ministry was empowered to appoint, discipline and promote its staff.

More important, the Central Bank of Nigeria (CBN) was removed from the Ministry of Finance and put directly under the Presidency. By so doing, the governor of the CBN had to work directly with the Office of the President. The implication is that, since the directors-general became political appointees and the CBN was also controlled directly by the Presidency, General Babangida could not but have greater supervisory role and "more direct hold on management of the country's dwindling financial resources."[4]

General Babangida's belief in the need to have a good control of government affairs was reinforced by the coup d' tats which, at different times, seriously threatened his regime. Recognising that his success, as well as the survival of his government, depended, to a great extent, on a strict

---

[4] *Africa Confidential*, vol. 29, no. 4, February 19, 1988, p. 1.

adherence to the return of power to civilians in 1992, he reduced the membership of the AFRC from 20 to 19. Besides, he tried to make a clear distinction between the AFRC and the government: only the defence minister was member of the AFRC in 1989. He made the police to be directly responsible to him to dissolving the Police Service Commission and taking "direct control of the force".[5]

He reorganised the machinery of government and the Presidency. The post of "Secretary to the Federal Military Government (FMG)" was re-created. In this context, the head of the civil service assumed responsibility only for establishment matters, staff discipline and service-related matters while the secretary to the FMG was, thenceforth, concerned with the design, implementation and co-ordination of policy.[6]

In regard to defence, the "Joint Chiefs of Staff" was created in the defence ministry. It was made up of the service chiefs and some very senior military officers whose main pre-occupation was to identify sources of internal and external threats to Nigeria. Embargo was placed on the procurement of new weapons while emphasis was placed on local training and on maintenance of old military equipment. Military personnel was reorganized and considerably cut down by 60 per cent. According to the General Saliu, many soldiers had exceeded their "run out date" and therefore would also have to be retired on the basis of "first come, first go" principle.[7] The cardinal aim

---

[5] *Africa Confidential*, vol. 30, no. 6. March 17 1989, p. 3.

[6] See President IBB's speech to ministers and permanent secretaries on The Budget and the Challenge of Policy Implementation, January 1986.

[7] See *New Nigerian*, 22 November, 1990, p. 1.

of the personnel cut was to reduce defence budget by about 20 per cent.

At the economic level, fundamental changes were made. the Babangida regime adopted self-defined structural adjustment programme (SAP) which many Nigerians saw as one of, if not, the most important landmark or "boldest economic policy action taken by any government in Nigeria since independence because of its radical approach to finding solution to the country's persistent economic crisis."[8]

It is important to recall that, before the introduction of SAP, which the IMF tried to directly impose on Nigeria on which the Babangida government officially rejected by the general requirements of which it assiduously implemented;[9] Nigeria's economy was in very bad shape.[10] So, SAP was more of a necessity the argument ran.

---

[8] See "Structural Adjustment in Nigeria: The Impact of the SFEM on the Economy," being Keynote Address by Alhaji A. Ahmed, Governor, Central Bank of Nigeria, delivered at the NIIA's seminar on Structural Adjustment Programme: The Impact of SFEM on the Economy, held on Tuesday, 30 June, 1987, p.1.

[9] The conditions included the devaluation of the naira by at least 60 per cent; cut in government expenditure; removal of consumer subsidies (food, petroleum products, etc.); trade liberalisation; removal of bureaucratic bottlenecks in the area of imports, foreign investments, import and exchange rates; price control, wage freeze, etc.

[10] There were several structural distortions in the economy: excessive emphasis on the export of crude oil which accounted for over 80 per cent of total government revenue and more than 95 per cent of total foreign exchange. As a result, little or no room was given for non-oil exports and development of the agricultural sector; the naira was over-valued; there was problem of import syndrome; dwindling foreign exchange earnings as a result of the decline in the demand for crude oil with effect from 1981. This created problems of balance of payments and credit unworthiness for the country. In fact, the

In conformity with the guidelines of SAP, the government declared a fifteen-month economic emergency during which the salaries of both the military and the civil servants were cut. The economy was liberalised. Government subsidies on oil and subventions to public parastatals were cut down. The government introduced a second tier foreign exchange market (SFEM) as the core element of the SAP on 29 September 1986. The aim was to:

> evolve a realistic market-determined exchange rate of the naira in order to...reduce the pressure on the balance of payments, effect rational resource allocation, eliminate the pervasive distortions in all the major sectors of the economy, reduce imports while stimulating the production of domestic substitutes and exports and pave way to a more reliant and sustainable growth.[11]

The exchange rate of the naira was allowed to be determined by market forces but with government-moderated regulations. In fact, here were two markets, one for the general public and another for the private sector.

In terms of transition to civil rule, General Babangida promised in his 1986 Budget Address that he would return power to a democratically-elected government in October 1990. Towards this end, he inaugurated a 15-person Political Bureau, chaired by Samuel J. Cookey, on 13 January, 1986. The Bureau was empowered to conduct a national debate on the political future of Nigeria. In its

---

stabilisation measures introduced in April 1982 failed to prevent the aggravation of the already worsening economic situation. This made the idea of SAP attractive as a new alternative economic policy option to General Babangida.

[11] Ibid., p. 4

report submitted to the government on March 27, 1987 the Bureau recommended a new political orientation for Nigeria. According to the Bureau, "the government should immediately initiate a comprehensive, coherent and sustained programme of social mobilisation and political education for the country" in order to awaken national consciousness, inculcate patriotism, and bring national vices (corruption, electoral malpractices, religious bigotry and ethnicity, etc.) under control.[12] The Bureau also recommended 1990 as the terminal date for the transition programme (1987-1990), the establishment of a directorate of social mobilisation and political education and some other agencies,[13] proclaim a new philosophy of government predicated on socialism, create area development committees and village with neighbourhood committees, conduct population census in 1988, lift the ban on politics in 1989 and organise gubernatorial and presidential elections in 1990.[14]

General Babangida, though agreed, did not fully comply with the recommendations. As a matter of fact, IBB gave Nigerians one of their greatest surprises on October 7, 1989 when he refused to choose any two political parties out of the six recommended to him by the National Electoral Commission (NEC). Earlier, thirteen political associations had applied for registration as political parties but the NEC recommended only six of them. What IBB simply did was

---

[12] See the *Report of the Political Bureau*, March 1987 (Abuja: Mamser, 1987) p. 209.

[13] They include the National Commission on Political Parties and Elections, National Population Commission, The Code of Conduct Bureau and Code of Conduct Tribunal, National Revenue and Fiscal Commission.

[14] *Report of the Political Bureau, op. cit.*, p. 226

to disband the thirteen political associations. In lieu, he created the Social Democratic Party (SDP) and the National Republican Convention (NRC). In this context, General Babangida explained that he was not prepared to resurrect the Second Republic. His non-preparedness clearly points to the desire to directly control the two political parties.

The implication was that, for different pretexts, General Babangida would not hand over power because the basis for it was never provided: elections could not be held until 1993. Even when the elections were successfully concluded in June 1993, the results of the elections were still annulled for unexplained reasons.

Prevention of unrest and insecurity

On the need to prevent unrest and insecurity, and particularly, having given the impression that he would pursue a new policy, IBB retired forty senior military officers on taking over power and named a younger (both in terms of age and rank) generation of officers as governors: one wing commander, one navy-captain, one navy commander, eight lieutenant-colonels, two majors, one police commissioner and three group captains. IBB's slogan was "the youth shall grow" or "this is the time for the youths". It should be stressed here that Babangidomania is predicated on the need for unwavering discipline and loyalty. It sought unconditional obedience of all the subordinates. When Commodore Ebitu Oko Ukiwe, the Chief of General Staff, disagreed in 1986 with general Babangida on the issue of protocol and precedence during the October 1 celebrations in Abuja, he got the AFRC to remove him and to name Rear Admiral (later, Admiral)

Augustus Aikhomu as his successor.[15] IBB distinguished between political appointment and military seniority and therefore argued that military seniority takes precedence:

> It is useful to also note that Babangidomania is also very aggressive: while, for instance, IBB tried to pamper the press and the academic community, on the one hand, he never failed to also condemn his critics in strong terms on the other. In a statement on "the imperative features of Nigerian foreign policy and the crisis in Liberia," General Babangida used abusive words when he commented about "those involved in false historical comparisons, intellectual intoxication and phantom analysis ..."[16]

General Babangida also portrayed his new outlook when he seriously threatened the northern Hausa-Fulani establishment by seeking to put an abrupt end to their monopoly of Nigerian politics: only four, out of the twenty-eight members of the then AFRC, can be said to be true northerners. In fact, the Sultan of Sokoto, who was surprised about IBB's successful coup d'etat, had to tell the 'President' that he (IBB) would have to relate to Allah through Sokoto. General Babangida replied the Sultan that he would like to "de-emphasize religion and ethnicity". This reply was "most frostily received in Sokoto".[17]

---

[15] *Africa Confidential*, vol. 27, no. 21, October 15, 1986, p. 1.

[16] See Federal Ministry of Information, Press Release, no. 790, October 31, 1990, p. 4

[17] *Africa Confidential*, vol. 27, no. 14, July 2, 1986, p. 1

The quest for legitimacy

In his quest for people's legitimacy, General Babangida capitalised on his predecessor's unpopularity to call for support for his regime. Shortly before he seized power, it should be recalled that Yoruba leaders, notably the retired senior army officers, had been suggesting a confederal system and had been complaining about "imposed leadership".[18] Apart from the socio-economic instability which IBB had to deal with, there were also problems of national unity and how to make the new administration look credible.

In order to garner the support of Nigerians and the friendship of the diplomatic community, General Babangida quickly held talks with virtually all the leaders of the military divisions in the country, as well as with the Nigeria police force. In his address to the officers of the armed forces and the Nigeria police on 27 September, 1985 IBB explained that "it is not possible to have all of you appointed into government jobs. That does not in any way mean that you cannot contribute." He, therefore, pleaded with them to set up "Services Advisory Council at various levels which will be charged with responsibilities for advising various commanders on tropical issues..."[19] General Babangida similarly sought the understanding and cooperation of both the diplomatic and academic communities respectively on August 30 and November 16,

---

[18] *Africa Confidential*, vol. 26, no. 16, July 31, 1985, pp. 3 and 4.
[19] See "Address by President IBB to Officers of the Armed Forces and Nigeria Police Force at the National Assembly Complex on 27th September, 1985;" see also Federal Ministry of Information and Culture, Press Release, no. 1647, September 27, 1985.

1985. He promised to respect all the internationally contracted obligations of Nigeria, adding that the then ongoing review of Nigeria's debt servicing-ratio did not imply non-readiness to settle Nigeria's debts.[20] In response to his pleas, the students, several associations and professional groups pledged their support and loyalty to him.[21]

What is more significant is that, in 1987, in order to further consolidate this initial support, IBB not only restored to Dr. Yakubu Gowon his rank of general in the Nigerian army but also backdated the restoration to February 1976 when he was stripped of his rank.[22] Additionally, he promoted, in early 1991, some already retired senior military officers, probably in an attempt to court the friendship of their followers still in the service who might have felt aggrieved by the way and manner of their retirement. He repealed Decree 4 of March 29, 1984 which protected public officials against "ridicule or disrepute" and also release all those detained without trial.

It is important to underscore the point that IBB also enjoyed international support. Mrs. Margaret Thatcher was the first western leader to send a congratulatory message to him. She was followed by Ronald Reagan who sent a 44-volume of books on constitutional law and human rights through a judicial delegation headed by Judge Arlin Adams, a member of the US Court of Appeal.[23] Ronald Reagan was

---

[20] Federal Ministry of Information and Culture, Press Release, no. 1478, August 30, 1985; *Daily Times*, August 31, 1985, p. 8

[21] See *National Concord*, December 25, 1985, p. 9; *Daily Sketch*, January 6, 1986, p. 1

[22] *Africa Research Bulletin* (Political Series), vol. 24, no. 10, 1987, p. 8675.

[23] *The Punch*, December 20, 1985, p. 7.

convinced that the "government under your leadership (IBB) will successfully guide Nigeria to the attainment of its vast potential."

The extent of the general support, as noted by Sidi A. Alli, is such that IBB became the first leader to have won the support of the *Nigerian Tribune*, to have earned a courtesy call from Dr. Nnamdi Azikiwe and to have the support of Dr. Tai Solarin, a social critic.[24] More important, a London daily, the *Independent*, noted in 1987 that "any young military officer who would try to grab power between now and the 1992 return to civilian rule would incur the wrath of the nation for interrupting that process."[25]

In general, babangidomania, as indirectly explained in 1990 by General Babangida himself, is not "pontifical". It is predicated on openness and largely influenced by public opinion. In his own words:

> [B]efore we took over in August 1985, the style of government and pronouncements by Government were pontifical. This Administration has changed all that and perhaps for ever. We can take credit for contributing to the renaissance of the culture of useful debates characteristic of the era of nationalist mobilisation of our people for independence. We have also challenged and provoked Nigerians - elite and ordinary folks - into speaking and declaring their position on issues that affect them and we have urged them to specify

---

[24] *Daily Times*, December 3, 1985, p. 18

[25] Quoted in *The Guardian* (Lagos), August 28, 1987, p. 16 and *Vanguard*, August 28, 1987, p. 1.

their expectations about public policy performance
of our leaders.[26]

From the foregoing, babangidomania discourages a confrontational attitude, encourages dialogue and 'debatocracy', consultation, compromise and appointment of younger generation of military officers into top government positions. It seeks popular support but does not tolerate any form of disobedience. It also encourages a prominent role for the First Lady in the governance of the country, especially as it relates to women and development. Mrs. Mariam Babangida was in charge of the Better Life for Rural Women programme which was government-sponsored and funded.

The external dimension

Openness, compromise and economic diplomacy

New foreign policy thrust

When IBB came to power, he inherited many unresolved problems:

a) deteriorating relationship with Britain, following the 1984 Umaru Dikko affair;

---

[26] See the Address delivered by General Babangida…on the occasion of the Chief of Army Staff Annual Conference on 22nd January, 1990; Extracts also in the Federal Ministry of Information, Press Release, no. 41, January 22, 1990, p. 2.

b) problems of poor funding of Nigeria's foreign policy programmes. For instance, only 1.52% of the total budgetary allocation was approved in 1984 for foreign policy programmes, compared with Senegal's 6%, Benin's 3.9%, Cote d'Ivoire's 3.3% and Zaire's 3%;[27]

c) closure of Nigeria's borders which had far-reaching effects for the immediate neighbours;

d) the general disaffection resulting from the April 15 1985 Order of the Federal Ministry of Internal Affairs, by which all illegal aliens in the country were asked to regularise their stay or leave the country before May 10, 1985. The illegal aliens were allowed to leave the country with a paltry sum of twenty naira only;[28]

e) the Buhari government was servicing the countries debt to the tune of 44 per cent and the state of the economy was really bad.

In the area of Nigeria's foreign relations, IBB noted that

> Nigeria's foreign policy in the last twenty months has been characterised by inconsistencies and incoherence...Our role as Africa's spokesman has diminished...the ousted military government conducted our external relations by a policy of retaliatory reaction.

---

[27] See Bolaji Akinyemi's Address to the Foreign Policy Conference, in *New Nigerian*, April 12, 1986, p. 7.

[28] *Africa Research Bulletin*, vol. 22, no. 4, May 15 1985, p. 7599 and vol. 22, no. 5, June 15, 1985, p. 7639.

More significantly, "Major-General Buhari was too rigid and uncompromising in his attitude to issues of national significance."[29]

From these complaints, the policy direction of IBB was clear. He would seek to remove the inconsistencies and incoherence characteristic of Nigeria's foreign policy; actively support Nigeria's role as Africa's spokesman; avoid retaliatory policies; avoid predicating Nigeria's diplomacy on vindictive considerations; discourage rigidity and promote understanding, pluralism and compromise in decision-making, as well as encourage new initiatives.

To a great extent, Nigeria's foreign policy was informed by these factors. Believing that "a government, be it civilian or military, should rule with the consent of the people it governs, if it is to reach its objective," General Babangida threw open all the different facets of Nigeria's foreign policy for examination and re-examination. A foreign policy conference was organised and held in Kuru, Jos, in April 1986.

Unlike the 1961 conference which was chaired by Dr. K.O. Mbadiwe (a public servant) and which was restricted to political parties, the Kuru Conference involved virtually all the different strata of Nigerian society. Besides, the Kuru Conference was organised by a committee headed by Haroun Adamu, chairman of *The Punch* group of newspapers, while Dr. Mbadiwe was involved in the 1961 Conference in his capacity as adviser on African affairs to Prime Minister Tafawa Balewa. As put by the economic committee of the Kuru 'All Nigeria Conference on Foreign

---

[29] See the text of IBB's Broadcast to the nation on the night of August 27, 1985 in the *Daily Sketch*, August 28, 1985, p. 3 and *West Africa*, no. 3549, September 2, 1985, pp. 1791-3

Policy', the 1961 Conference ignored substantive questions relating to the primary level of existence of Nigerians and was simply designed to allow "radicals to let off steam…" Consequently, the 1985 conference was generally perceived as very important, all-embracing and useful.

The 1986 Kuru Conference recommended an activist role in world affairs for Nigeria. It anchored Nigeria's new foreign policy thrusts on building a strong, self-reliant, modern economy and creating a formidable military-industrial complex. The conference believed that the foundation of a true non-alignment policy is an independent national economy and that "the development of independent foreign policy for Africa on the basis of non-alignment can be realised if there is an independent economic base." Similarly, it was argued, a sound economic base was necessary for the security and defence of the country.[30]

This recommendation conforms to the primary pursuit of General Babangida. It is no surprise, therefore, that Nigeria's foreign policy was mainly predicated on economic diplomacy under General Babangida. While Professor Bolaji Akinyemi, his first foreign minister, gave greater saliency to the economic component of Nigeria's foreign relations, his successor, General Ike Nwachukwu, made economic diplomacy the main thrust of Nigeria's foreign policy. Laudable as it was, the objectives of economic diplomacy could not be attained because of the hostility of the international community to Nigeria's unstable polity, the major cause of which was ascribed to

---

[30] See the Report of the Political and Economic Committees of the All Nigeria Conference on Foreign Policy, 6th - 13th April, 1986, NIPSS, Kuru, pp. 209 et s.

military dictatorship. However, international response to it was still mixed.[31]

Nigeria sought international support for her structural adjustment programme. Nigeria's official creditors made it clear in December 1985 that an agreement with the International Monetary Fund was a precondition to rescheduling of Nigeria's debt. In fact, negotiations on Nigeria's request for a loan of UK£2.5 billion had earlier been suspended.[32] When Sir Geoffrey Howe, the British Foreign Secretary, visited Nigeria in September 1985, he said Nigeria should take an IMF loan before medium-term credit cover by Britain's Export Credits Guarantee Department (EGCD) could be resumed. In his words, such a loan "would help us (Britain) to give more help to Nigeria."[33]

In this context, the IMF imposed 'conditionalities' which Nigerians rejected: immediate 60% devaluation of the naira, cancellation of oil subsidies and removal of import restrictions. The position of the IBB government was to have a "precedent-setting agreement which would allow for a rescheduling of debts payments falling due without prior agreement with the IMF."[34] But Nigerians were opposed to the idea. General Babangida subjected the

---

[31] Bola A. Akinterinwa, "External Response to Nigeria's Economic Diplomacy," *Nigerian Journal of International Studies*, vol. 15, nos. 1 and 2, November 1991, pp. 112-135.

[32] *Africa Research Bulletin* (Economic Series), vol. 23, no. 2, March 31, 1986, p. 8126.

[33] *Africa Research Bulletin* (Economic Series), vol. 22, no. 8, September 30, 1985, pp. 7880-7882.

[34] *Africa Research Bulletin* (Economic Series), vol. 23, no. 4, May 31, 1986, p. 8207 B.

issue to debate. However, on December 12, 1985, in a television address, he said

> the path of honour and the essence of democratic patriotism lies in discontinuing the negotiations with the IMF for a support loan...This is clearly the will of the majority of our people on this issue...We will continue to honour our legitimate and clearly established financial obligations within the limits of our financial resources.[35]

In order to reconcile the exigencies of the foreign creditors with the opposition of Nigerians to IMF conditionalities, IBB accepted the rejection of an IMF loan but implemented all the IMF conditionalities as imposed by the IMF but ostensibly by fellow Nigerians. Thus, the element of imperialism was no more an issue and the rescheduling of Nigeria's debts was also made possible, especially that the IMF had given its formal approval to an agreement reached with Nigeria in 1986 which, in principle, allowed Nigeria a SDR 650m ($823m) facility and to which the rescheduling agreements with other creditors were tied.[36]

In fact, Nigeria reached a tentative agreement with the commercial bank creditors on November 20, 1986 but the terms of the agreement were not satisfactory to Nigeria. Nigeria however "agreed to conclude the negotiations...in order not to jeopardise the World Bank loan and perhaps

---

[35] *Africa Research Bulletin* (Economic Series), vol. 24, no. 1, February 28, 1987, p. 8558 C.
[36] *Africa Research Bulletin* (Economic Series), vol. 24, no. 1, February 28, 1987, p. 8558 C.

the whole economic reform programme."[37] Apparently, IBB's attitude was that of compromise which paid off: the commercial bank creditors later brought to an end the eighteen months of negotiations on November 23, 1987 by signing a US$4.2 billion rescheduling and now loan package with Nigeria.[38] Besides, Nigeria was also able to sign on April 5, 1988 bilateral agreements rescheduling debts owed to Japan, Germany, Sweden, Italy, France, etc.[39] The international support for General Babangida was to the extent that smaller creditors had to complain about the favoured treatment being given to Nigeria.[40] IBB's openness, compromise, if not an outright tactical submissiveness, enabled international understanding of Nigeria's problems.

What should be underscored here is that, while General Babangida was showing readiness to sign agreements rescheduling Nigeria's debts, he was, at the same time, asking for debt reduction or debt forgiveness and to which the creditors generally showed no sympathy. Nigeria was considered rich and that she should eschew economic 'squandermania' if her economy was to be revamped.

---

[37] See the main conditions in *Africa Research Bulletin* (Economic Series), vol. 23, no. 11, December 31, 1986, pp. 8478-9

[38] *Africa Research Bulletin* (Economic Series), vol. 24, no. 11, December 31, 1987, p. 8931 AB.

[39] *Africa Research Bulletin*, vol. 25, no. 3, April 30, 1988, p. 9077; vol. 27, no. 1, February 28, 1990, p. 9842; vol. 26, no. 7, August 31, 1989, p. 9647; vol. 26, no. 11, December 31, 1989 p. 9778 9; vol. 27, no. 2, March 31, 1990, p. 9880 BC; and vol. 27, no. 5, June 30, 1990, p. 9985 BC.

[40] *Africa Research Bulletin*, vol. 26, no. 2, March 31, 1987, p. 9475.

Strengthening Nigeria's leadership role

Consistent with an activist role recommended by the Kuru Conference for Nigeria, the technical aid corps (TACS) programme was created, with the main objective of providing assistance to African countries. It was established at a time Nigeria was in a deep economic crisis and when the contributions of the professionals who were to be sent abroad were also required at home. Similarly, the Concert of Medium Powers (CMP) was also organised in March 1987. Although the CMP, which changed its name to Lagos Forum, attracted much heated debate,[41] and has, probably as a result of lack of domestic support, been discouraged, the fact remains that it was designed to enable Nigeria play an increasing activist role in world affairs, and notably in the African sphere.

Indeed, Nigeria was able to play an important role: Nigeria and Brazil co-sponsored the first UNH resolution on the South Atlantic, declaring it a "zone of peace". It was, again, at the instance of Nigeria that the "South African defence fund" was established by the Eighth Non-Aligned Summit held in Harare in August 1986. The summit also adopted Nigeria's proposal that there should be a stockpile of relief goods for the "frontline states" in anticipation of the effects of sanctions being taking against Pretoria. More importantly, the Babangida government made special efforts to secure the election of many Nigerians into top positions in international organisations. Of note are the

---

[41] Bola A. Akinterinwa, "The Lagos Forum and the Medium Powers Debate," *International Problems, Society and Politics*, vol. XXVIII, no. 52 (1-2), 1987, pp. 57-68.

returning unopposed of Ambassador Brownson Dede as OAU assistant secretary-general in 1987,[42] even if he was voted out in 1995 of this position because of increasing international hostility against Nigeria; the election of Professor Godwin Obasi as the secretary-general of the World Meteorology Organisation, election of Nigeria's attorney-general, Prince Bola Ajibola as a member of the UN International Law Commission, election of Malam Yaya Aliyu to the executive board of the UNESCO, election of Major-General Joseph Garba as president of the 44th Session of the UN General Assembly in 1989, election of Chief Emeka Anyaoku as the first African secretary-general of the Commonwealth in 1990, election of Alhaji Rilwanu Lukman as secretary-general of the OPEC, etc.

It should be mentioned also that Nigeria sponsored General Olusegun Obasanjo for the position of the UN secretary-general in 1991. The failure of General Obasanjo was principally ascribed to Nigeria's military dictatorship.

Promotion of cordial relationship

In general, Nigeria maintained a very cordial attitude towards her foreign partners which served as a basis for the building of a mutually rewarding relationship. Britain's ECGD fully restored cover facilities, suspended in 1984,

---

[42] Foreign Minister Bolaji Akinyemi saw his re-election as very significant because the position of OAU Assistant Secretary-General has always been held by a Nigerian since the inception of the organisation. See A. B. Akinyemi's "Foreign Policy Self-Assessment," *Nigerian Statesman*, August 27, 1987, pp. 7 and 10; and *Nigerian Tribune*, October 6, 1987, p. 9.

for Nigeria, on July 28, 1987.[43] In spite of the controversy surrounding the British Consular Office on Awolowo Road, Ikoyi, Mrs. Margaret Thatcher still paid official visit to Nigeria in January 1988, a visit General Babangida returned in May 1989 and during which he was honoured with the Knight Grand Cross of the Order of Bath (GCB) by Queen Elizabeth II. In fact, IBB, who believed that Mrs. Thatcher was a "wonderful woman and probably one of the greatest leaders we have in the world," de-emphasized the extradition of Alhaji Umaru Dikko, Adisa Akinloye and others and also lifted the ban placed in 1979 on British Petroleum's oil activities in Nigeria. The oil company was allowed to return as a fresh company and its new operations were not to be linked to its past operations in any way.[44] Similarly, the British Commonwealth Development Corporation, an investment company which was compelled to leave in 1976 as a result of Nigeria's Enterprises Promotion Decree, was also authorised to begin operations in Nigeria.[45]

Relations with France were considerably improved. In spite of the attachment of Nigeria's aircrafts in France, General Babangida officially visited Paris and signed on February 27, 1990 an agreement on the avoidance of double taxation and prevention of fiscal evasion with respect to taxes on income and capital gains and another agreement on the mutual encouragement and protection of investment for an initial period of ten years. Besides, when General Babangida was suffering from radiculopathy, his medical expenses at the American Hospital in Neuilly-sur-Soine

---

[43] *Africa Research Bulletin*, vol. 24, no. 7, August 31, 1987, p. 8776-7.
[44] *The Guardian* (Lagos), May 16, 1991, p. 1.
[45] *The Guardian* (Lagos), May 22, 1991, p. 28.

were borne by the French government. The gesture is an expression of the newly-found rapprochement between Francois Mitterrand and IBB.

Nigeria moved closer to the United States under General Babangida. When the US secretary of state, George Shultz, visited Nigeria on January 12, 1987 he admitted having held "the most constructive set of discussions with Nigerians for…six years" while General Babangida expressed the hope that Mr. Schultz's visit symbolised the common values of both countries.[46]

Nigeria's relations with western Europe were also quite good in spite of some thaw, like the 1988 toxic waste imbroglio between Nigeria and Italy. Nigeria's economic diplomacy brought many Asian countries closer to Nigeria. The case of Japan was most significant. Probably in compensation for Nigeria's persistent deficit balance of trade with Japan, Japan increased the number of her grants and technical assistance programmes to Nigeria.[47] In fact, Japanese involvement in the execution of important projects in Nigeria (petroleum refinery in Port Harcourt, National Fertilizer Company in Onne, NEPA projects, Delta IV gas-turbine project at Ughelli, eradication of guinea worm in Nigeria, etc.) was tremendous to the extent that General Babangida, on August 30, 1989, conferred the National Honour of Commander of the Order of the Niger

---

[46] *Africa Research Bulletin* (Political Series), vol. 24, no. 1, February 15, 1987, p. 8380.

[47] *Africa Research Bulletin*, vol. 26, no. 4, May 31, 1989, p. 9553; vol. 27, no. 3 April 30, 1990, p. 9928 and vol. 27, no. 11, November 16 - December 15, 1990, p. 10205.

(CON) on the Japanese Ambassador, Mr. Mitsuro Donowaki.[48]

While Nigeria maintained her cordial relations with and commitment to the Organisation of African Unity, she showed special interest in the ECOWAS by assuming more financial and more responsibilities. When the ECOWAS council of ministers revised the architectural design of the Community's new secretariat in June 1986, thus also increasing the cost of the building from $16.5 to $22 million, Nigeria accepted to contribute the difference of $5.6 million.[49] Again, when little interest was shown in the chairmanship of the ECOWAS, General Babangida accepted responsibility: he was re-elected to an unprecedented third term in 1987. Nigeria was also one of the main architects of ECOMOG, the organisation's military wing, and its eventual involvement in the Liberian crisis.

At the level of the immediate neighbours, efforts were made to resolve the problem of the Bakassi peninsula amicably. As a result of several Camerounian incursions into Nigerian villages in 1987, and following Nigerian government's order to all the governors of states sharing borders with the neighbours, asking them to "take military reprisals against any belligerent neighbouring country." President Paul Biya sent his information and culture minister, Mr. Mbombo Njoya with a note to General Babangida. This was quickly reciprocated by the six-day official visit of Major-General Sani Abacha, then the Army Chief of Staff. During the visit, the possibility of joint

---

[48] *Daily Times* and *New Nigerian*, August 31, 1989, pp. 1 and 14, and 1 and 3 respectively.

[49] *Africa Research Bulletin*, vol. 24, no. 1, February 28, 1987, p. 8537.

border patrols was discussed.[50] General Babangida also visited Cameroun from 8th to 11th December, 1987. In spite of their joint communiqué, by which both countries promised to take steps to prevent a recurrence of border skirmishes, especially through joint border patrols, Cameroun still renewed her incursions.[51]

Nigeria-Equatorial Guinea relations under General Babangida were made uneasy as a result of the revelation of the presence of some white South Africans in Malabo, who, allegedly, were there to launch an aid programme and assist in some development projects. Nigeria asked for the expulsion of the South Africans for security reasons. Nigeria's mistrust towards Equatorial Guinea was heightened on discovering in May 1988 that the South Africans had not left or had returned to the country. In an attempt to find a lasting solution to the Malabo issue, General Babangida visited Malabo in June 1988, not only to make Nigerian presence felt there by laying the foundation of a new Nigerian Chancery in Malabo but by also giving a five million naira aid package to the country. The aid included the construction of a 52-bed modern polyclinic, an 11-clasroom high brow school and university scholarships to thirteen Equatorial Guineans.[52]

More significantly, in an attempt to address the problem from a sub regional perspective, General Babangida proposed the establishment of a 'Gulf of Guinea Commission,' to be made up of Gabon, Cameroun. Sao

---

[50] *Africa Research Bulletin* (Political Series), vol. 24, no. 10, November 15, 1987, p. 8660 B.

[51] *Africa Research Bulletin* (Political Series), vol. 24, no. 12, January 15, 1988, p. 8721 BC; the *Guardian* (Lagos), May 20, 1991, p. 1 and May 29, 1991, p. 13.

[52] *Africa Research Bulletin*, vol. 25, no. 5, June 30, 1980, p. 9132 BC.

Tome and Principe, Equatorial Guinea and Nigeria. All these countries, the Nigerian leader advocated, "must gratefully acknowledge our endowment in the Gulf of Guinea which is a gift of nature to all our States." Consequently, "the overlapping exclusive economic zones of states in the Gulf must not be seen as a source of unhealthy competition and potential conflicts," he added. This posture clearly points to good neighbourliness.

On a general note, Nigeria's behaviour in international relations from August 1985 through 1993 was primarily predicated on the desire to revamp the economy as quickly as possible. Nigeria's foreign policy was not reactionary. Babangidomania was not rigid *per se*. Nigeria's foreign relations and international image witnessed a lot of improvement and goodwill.

However, 'babangidomania' had one major weakness which seemed to have neutralized most of the gains scored before General Babangida became wrapped up in the glory of the manifest support at home and foreign policy success abroad. It is at this juncture that 'babangidocracy' as a legacy has also become a burden for Nigeria.

The problems of IBB's legacy

The main problem of babangidomania is that General Babangida consciously or otherwise, tolerated general indiscipline at the home level to the extent that he not only found it difficult to control official corruption but also preferred to sit tight rather than seek to hand over power to an elected government.

By the time he was forced out of power in 1993, he had already succeeded in bequeathing a crippling legacy of indiscipline, largely built on a 'settlement culture' and institutional corruption and on the use of brute force against his critics and opponents.

General Babangida, one source said, found it difficult to displease people, especially his friends. He seemed to have an attitude which sought to show gratitude to all and sundry who might have helped him in one way or the other. He tried to 'settle' differences and other problems with money. In light of this, it became difficult for General Babangida to seriously control official corruption. The immediate effect was that most Nigerians also took a cue from it. The 'ten percentage culture' became generalised. In fact nothing could work without money. Nigerians lost their Nigerianness and often think in terms of their own survival at the detriment of that of the country. In fact, when Nigerians, especially receptionists and law enforcement agents, jokingly ask for Family Support Programme (FSP), which is a re-incarnation of the Better Life Programme, they directly are asking for bribe to support their own family.

In the private sector, business transactions were characterised by 'advance fee fraud' popularly known as '419' and embezzlements. When public buildings were gutted by fire, it was often the accounts departments that were first affected.

Besides, General Babangida was no longer interested in justice but probably in its perversion: he installed Alhaji Ibrahim Dasuki rather than the legitimate successor and people's choice, Alhaji Muhammadu Maccido.[53]

---

[53] Eventually, the Government of General Sani Abacha approved the removal of Alhaji Ibrahim Dasuki in April 1996 and the installation of Alhaji Mohammadu Maccido Abubakar III as the 19th Sultan of

Additionally, he ruined all his efforts and electoral ingenuity, characteristic of the electoral process by annulling the results of the presidential elections of June 12, 1993 which further divided the country and rekindled ethnic suspicion. Generally, the annulment was interpreted to be an anti-people decision. Since the annulment, Nigeria has been operating on a keg of gun powder and in a new environment of increasing insecurity and terrorist acts.

Although General Abacha inherited the aftermath of the annulment and is still grappling with the disunity and insecurity created by the annulment of the results of the June 12, 1993 presidential elections, it is still not clear whether a stable political order can be possible without meaningfully addressing the issue of June 12. What is above controversy is that the June 12 saga was Babangida-created.

In a nutshell, the Babangida who started well and enjoyed popular support at the initial stage became an object of contempt and a *persona non grata* at the end of it all. As at today, Nigeria is still seriously suffering from the reckless indiscipline which babangidomania accommodated. Under General Sani Abacha, indiscipline was yet to be effectively controlled. Many of the institutional structures and policies bequeathed by IBB (DIFFRI, MAMSER, Road Safety, People's Bank, community banks, etc.) have either been cancelled, transformed or maintained. For instance, the Better Life Programme, as noted earlier, was reorganised into a Family Support Programme under Mrs. Mariam Abacha), etc.

Sokoto on Monday, 17th June, 1996. See *The Guardian* and *This Day* of June 18, 1996, p. 1.

These points to the fact that some major aspects of IBB legacy will sooner or later, be overtaken by new legacies.

In an attempt to restore sanity and discipline and put embezzlement and political chicanery at bay, General Abacha promulgated the failed banks and failed contractors decrees, etc. General Abacha's effort has produced positive results. However, the promulgation of the decrees constitutes a manifestation of the complexity of the problem of public embezzlement and general corruption which had been a feature of the Nigerian polity before General Babangida took over power but which was sharply generalized during his tenure in power.

Concluding remarks

In conclusion, it is safe to note that IBB lost everything he achieved for one major reason. The Political Bureau made it clear to IBB in 1987 that

> ...corruption and indiscipline are two of the most serious problems which have confronted the Nigerian political process since independence. These twin problems reached scandalous dimensions during the last civilian regime. Nigerians are indeed unanimous in believing that any effort at erecting a new political order which does not tackle these twin problems of corruption and indiscipline is bound to fail. The Bureau shares this opinion.[54]

---

[54] See *The Report of the Political Bureau*, *op. cit.*, p. 215.

In spite of this warning, the twin problems were allowed to increase in intensity and scope under IBB.

One way out of this dilemma is for Nigerian leaders to first learn to accept the temporariness of life, of their stay in power, of the uselessness of an undesired and undeserved long stay in power. The desire to stay in power by all mean lubricates the engine of indiscipline and corruption. Even if the desire is good in itself, the goodness cannot be relevant and useful if the desire is not predicated on an acceptable time-frame to relinquish power. In more advanced countries, good leaders are able to trace a line of development in one term of four years for their people even if the full implementation of their agenda is allowed to begin in their second term of office. If a leader cannot do his best in two terms of four or five years, the likelihood of his performing better after ten years is remote. General Babangida organised, on the one hand, and disorganised, on the other, and by so doing, created a lull which Nigerians are now unsuccessfully grappling with.

Malthouse Monographs on Africa

Editor: Dafe Otobo, DPhil (Oxford),
Professor, University of Lagos, Lagos, Nigeria

Advisory Editorial Board

Malthouse Monographs on Africa

Malthouse Monographs on Africa are peer-reviewed works on Africa covering the six main areas of a) social sciences and development studies; b) history, law and international relations; c) environmental and agricultural studies; d) gender, refugee and conflict studies; e) strategic and defence studies; and f) labour and trades unions.

The monographs are intended to provide an arena for free contestation of ideas and as outlet for research and empirical studies on Africa in the areas indicated above. The monographs thus have no links with, nor funded by, any government or political party. Nor do the views expressed in them represent those of the editorial board.

Works for consideration may be of purely theoretical, or historical or applied in nature or policy-oriented. Such may be sent directly to the Editor as electronic files (dafeotobo2002@yahoo.co.uk) in Microsoft Word Rich Text format, or to the publishers (malthouse_press@yahoo.com}. Diskettes and hardcopies may also be sent to the publishers at the address on the imprint page. The aim is to publish accepted works within three months.

Malthouse Monographs on Africa
Numbers 1-9

Guest Series Editor: Dayo Oluyemi-Kusa
Director, External Conflict Prevention & Resolution, Institute for Peace and Conflict Resolution, The Presidency, Abuja, Nigeria

.

- Rotimi T. Suberu, *Institutional structure and process of government in Nigeria, 1985-1993*
- R. A. Akindele, *Federalism under General Babangida's administration in Nigeria*
- Dele Olowu & Kunle Awotokun, *Local government and the IBB administration*
- Cyril Obi, *The Nigerian private sector under adjustment and crisis 1985-1993*
- Bola A. Akinterinwa, *General Ibrahim Babangida's legacy: the domestic and international dimensions*
- Nereus I. Nwosu, *Nigeria's foreign policy under General Babangida*
- Antonia T. Oko-Osi, *Corruption and corrupt practices: institutionalization and legitimation under the Babangida Administration*
- Oyeleye Oyediran & Babafemi Badejo, *The military and democracy in Nigeria: the Political Bureau Report*
- Adekunle Amuwo, *Politics of the annulment of June 12 presidential election in Nigeria*

Malthouse Press Limited
43 Onitana Street, Off Stadium Hotel Road,
Surulere, Lagos, Lagos State
E-mail: malthouse_press@yahoo.com
malthouse_lagos@yahoo.co.uk
Tel: +234 (01) -773 53 44; 0802 364 2402

© Malthouse Monographs on Africa 2007
First Published 2007
ISBN 978 023 231 1

Distributors:
African Books Collective Ltd
Email: abc@africanbookscollective.com
Website: http://www.africanbookscollective.com

Guest Editor's comment

All the Monographs in this series attempt to explore and document events, policies and impact of the General Ibrahim Babangida-led military regime in Nigeria, covering the period 1985 to 1993. These contributions were originally for a book edited by me on that regime but other considerations, especially that of comprehensiveness of coverage of arguably the most momentous phase in Nigeria's post-Civil War socio-political development, led to the shelving of that idea. It was thought that a more useful scope or coverage might be achieved through a continuing development of Monographs on different facets of Nigerian society under this regime – a feat which may only be possible in a book so voluminous and whose cost might be such as to be out of the reach of the intended audience.

I should like to thank all the contributors who have waited this long to see their work in print, a fate that is unlikely to befall the contributors of the other titles currently in preparation. I am grateful to the publishers for including these titles in Malthouse Monographs for Africa family.

Dayo Oluyemi-Kusa

Contents

Nigeria's foreign policy under General Babangida

Nereus I. Nwosu PhD
Department of Political Science
University of Ibadan
Ibadan, Nigeria

No. 6

Introduction

Foreign policy means the "decisions and actions which involve to some appreciable extent relations between one state and others."[55] This definition informed the position of John Spanier and Eric Uslaner when they contend that the conduct of foreign policy aims at the "safe guarding the nation's security so that life may be preserved and enjoyed."[56] The deduction from these is that foreign policy deals essentially with relations external to states. By implication, it involves the actions and interactions of states within the international system. It is, therefore, necessary for states to use their foreign policy objectives to project the image of their countries externally, and build international goodwill. It is for this reason that states formulate principles and objectives that should guide their foreign policy formulation and implementation. These principles and objectives in states' foreign policy usually endure for long. What usually changes are the tactics and strategies adopted in the achievement of these goals by different regimes.

Nigeria as a sovereign state has provided the principles and objectives that should guide her foreign policy. These principles and objectives which were enunciated by the first prime minister of the country, Sir Abubakar Tafawa Balawa has remained consistent in spite of changes in regime. Some of these include non-alignment, multi-lateralism,

---

[55] Joseph Frankel, *The making of foreign policy: an analysis of Decision-making* London: Oxford University Press, 1963, p. 1.

[56] John Spanier & Eric M. Uslaner, *American Foreign Policy Making and the Democratic Dilemmas California*: Brooks/Cole Publishing Company, 1989, p. l.

equality of states, non-interference in internal affairs of states, respect for independence and territorial integrity of all states and Africa-centre-piece- policy.[57]

The importance which successive Nigerian governments attach to the country's foreign policy goals has informed the need for these regimes to articulate their external relations immediately on assumption of office or even before fully taking over power. Sir Abubakar for instance took out time to enunciate his government's foreign policy objectives to the Nigerian parliament even before independence on 20 August, 1960. Subsequent regimes have followed suit.

Foreign policy has indeed become fundamental that military regimes now capitalise on the failures of their predecessors in that field to secure legitimacy and justification of coup d'etat. General Babangida, for instance justified his overthrow of the Buhari's regime partly on the ground that the latter's foreign policy was 'negative and retaliatory' especially to African states. The negative and retaliatory' foreign policy of the Buhari regime centred mainly on the closure of Nigerian borders, the expulsion of illegal aliens and the diplomatic row between the country and Britain. It also concerned the regime's lack of progress in negotiation with the International Monetary Fund (IMF) over loan facilities to Nigeria.[58]

It is on this basis that this chapter examines the extent to which Babangida's foreign policy attempted to move

---

[57] R. A. Akindele & Bassey A. Ate, Nigeria's Foreign Policy, 1986--2000 AD: background to the reflections on the views from Kuru," *Nigerian Journal of International Affairs*, vol. 12 Nos. 1&2, 1986, P13; & N.I. Nwosu, The structure of foreign policy making, PhD. Dept. of Political Science, University of Ibadan, 1991, pp. 33-39.

[58] *Newswatch* [Lagos] 9 September, 1985, p. 19.

away from being a 'negative and retaliatory' one. In order to achieve this, specific case studies shall be examined. These include international reconciliation, settlement of disputes, projection of Nigerian and African personality, economic and social justice and accommodation of international institutions.

International reconciliation

Early in the life of his administration, General Babangida demonstrated the need for reconciliation between Nigeria and countries with which she has had problems especially during the twenty months tenure of Buhari. The regime began by finding accommodation with Britain. It would be recalled that there had existed a rupture in diplomatic relations between the two countries following the abortive attempt by some Nigerians and Israelis to crate Umaru Dikko, Nigeria's Second Republic transport minister to the country for trial over his alleged abuse of office during his ministerial tenure. The failed kidnap attempt led to the recalling of the High Commissioners of the two countries by their governments. Following from this, the two countries maintained some diplomatic distance.[59]

In order to facilitate reconciliation between the two countries, General Babangida's regime decided to initiate diplomatic effort at all levels of government between the two states. The effort resulted in several visits either between the foreign ministers of both countries, special

---

[59] Ibrahim A. Gambari, *Theory and Reality in Foreign policy making* Atlantic Highlands, NJ: Humanities Press International, 1989, pp.1 42-144.

delegates of the heads of government or the heads of government themselves. For instance, Nigeria's former minister of external affairs, Bolaji Akinyemi and his British counterpart, Geoffrey Howe exchanged visits to find ways of resolving the differences. The visits facilitated a rapprochement and culminated in an exchange of visits by the two heads of government. The British Prime Minister, Margaret Thatcher, visited Nigeria twice in 1988 and 1989, while General Babangida, Nigeria's military president went to Britain in 1989. During these visits, bilateral matters were discussed, especially how the two countries could improve on the existing relations. The rapprochement was also demonstrated with the conferment of the British national award of the Grand Cross of the order of Bath on Babangida by Queen Elizabeth II. In a gesture of reciprocation, Babangida conferred the Grand Commander of the Federal Republic on the British monarch.[60]

In resolving to improve diplomatic relations with Britain, the Babangida regime was mindful of the important role the British government could play in the country's debt rescheduling with both the London and the Paris clubs. This is because Britain is an important member of these clubs. Again, the Babangida regime was also counting on the fact that since Britain is a major trading partner of Nigeria, the latter needed to improve diplomatic relations with the former so as to enhance her economic benefits from such transactions. This is especially so in a situation where the Nigeria economy is recessed and there was the need to resuscitate it through foreign investments. It should be noted that British companies such as the United African Company and Shell Petroleum Development Company

---

[60] *Newswatch* [Lagos] 22 May, 1989, pp. 24-25.

dominated the Nigerian commercial and petroleum sectors. The only way, therefore, to make these companies more committed to the resuscitation of the Nigerian economy and attract new ones, the Nigerian regime believed was through the normalisation of the strained diplomatic relations between her and Britain. As Asobie rightly pointed out, Babangida's structural adjustment programme (SAP) is basically 'a diplomacy directed primarily at maximising the inflow of foreign investment, enhancing the prospects of promoting Nigeria's export and facilitating the rescheduling of Nigeria's external debts.'[61]

The attempt to reconcile with Britain did not, however, make the Babangida regime loose sight of the fact that national pride and prestige are important in a state's foreign policy. The regime, therefore, did not fail to apply the stick when situation demanded it. This could be seen from the way the Babangida government handled the issue of a new British visa office which was located very close to Dodan Barracks, the then seat of the Nigerian government. The Nigerian government despite all entreaties ordered the immediate closure of the office. It was only opened after the British government had given the Nigerian government certain assurances. In the same light, the Babangida regime on 29 January 1987 served a twelve-month notice on Britain to the effect that the bilateral air agreement between the two countries, which gave the British Caledonian Airways advantage over the Nigerian Airways, will be

---

[61] H. Assisi Asobie "Nigeria: Economic Diplomacy and National Interest, An Analysis of the Policies of Nigeria's External Economic Relations, with Special Reference to Ibrahim Babangida's Administration", paper presented at the 16th Annual Conference of the Nigerian Society of International Affairs held at NIIA, Nov. 5-6, 1990, p. 20.

terminated.[62] Apart from this, the Babangida administration in response to the British demand that the Nigerian Airways staff should procure entry visa to Britain insisted on a similar condition for the British Caledonian crew. This forced the British government to withdraw such order.[63]

In spite of this, the Babangida regime still showed great caution in its dealings with Nigeria's main trading partners who were mainly countries of Western Europe and North America. The regime acted in such a way as not to antagonise these states. It thus tolerated several acts of bad faith by these countries. For instance, when the United States bombed Libya in 1986, the Nigerian government did not react immediately by condemning the United States despite the country's 'Africa centrepiece' policy. Even when it did react following public disenchantment over the regime's nonchalant attitude, the then Nigerian minister of external affairs, Bolaji Akinyemi contended that 'we must not and cannot allow states which of their own free will adopt policies that lead to crisis to assume that Nigeria will automatically be dragged into that crisis That is not a position of leadership, that is a position of subservience.'[64] This position by the Babangida regime might have been informed by the administration's perception that it needed the United States and its western allies more than Libya in her attempt to resuscitate the Nigerian economy.

Again, the Babangida regime demonstrated its positive disposition to countries of the West by the frequent travels

---

[62] *This Week* (Lagos] 2 March, 1987, pp. 13-17.
[63] Ibid., p. 13.
[64] A. B. Akinyemi "Welcome address by the Minister of External Affairs at the formal opening of the all-Nigeria Conference on foreign policy," Kuru, 7th April 1986, *Nigeria: Bulletin on Foreign Affairs* vol. 1 No 1 June 1986, p6.

of Nigerian officials to these states. Even President Babangida travelled to some of these states, but failed to pay official visit to the United States due to disagreement on the date for the visit. During the visits embarked upon by the Nigerian officials, attempts were made to impress these western states of Nigeria's goodwill to them. Hence, Asobie posited that:

> In Europe, Akinyemi strived to make Nigeria command the respect of the governments and peoples of Britain, France and the United States; Nwachukwu sought to evoke the sympathy and obtain the mercy of the governments and the business community, for Nigeria's economic plight.[65]

The need for reconciliation also led the Babangida government to restore diplomatic relations with Israel. This was in spite of the hostile domestic opinion particularly from the country's Muslim population. It would be recalled that the preceding Buhari regime had maintained that the basis for rapprochement with Israel did not exist. It even went to the extent of punishing two traditional rulers for fraternising with Tel Aviv.[66]

In attempting to restore diplomatic relations with Israel, the Babangida regime knew it needed tact. This the regime applied by taking tentative steps initially. The regime became emboldened when it felt that enough domestic support had been built for its purpose. It thus, came out to openly interact with Israeli officials at very

---

[65] Asobie, *loc. cit.*, p. 27.
[66] Gambari, *loc. cit.*, p. 171.

high levels.[67] These finally resulted in the restoration of diplomatic relations between Nigeria and Israel at ambassadorial level on 4 May 1992.

The need for the restoration in diplomatic relations between Nigeria and Israel became compelling because the Babangida regime saw the latter as a country that could help resuscitate the nation's recessed economy. This is particularly in the field of agriculture where Israel had proved very helpful during the First Republic.[68] Again, the Babangida administration felt that it was loosing the initiative to other African countries that were already re-establishing diplomatic relations with Israel. Such countries include Cameroon, Central African Republic, Cote D'Ivoire, Egypt, Gabon, Kenya, Togo and Zaire.[69] It was, therefore, partly to maintain her self-imposed mission of an African giant and a regional power that the regime decided to move ahead of the Organisation of African Unity [OAU] in the restoration of diplomatic relations with Israel. In addition, the rapprochement was also necessitated by the changing international order where old foes were becoming friends and old ideological alliances were been dismantled. Also, the thaw in relationship was essentially only in the diplomatic front. At least, prior to the restoration in diplomatic relations, Nigeria and Israel were co-operating in the economic realm as many Israeli companies were participating in several government projects in Nigeria.[70]

---

[67] *Newswatch* (Lagos) 18 May, 1992.
[68] Olajide Aluko, *Essays on Nigerian Foreign Policy,* London: George Allen & Unwin, 1981, p. 83.
[69] *Newswatch* (Lagos] 6 March, 1989, p. 22.
[70] N.I. Nwosu 'Influence of Domestic Factors on Nigeria-Israeli Rapprochement,' *Annals of the Social Science Council of Nigeria* (forthcoming).

Nigerian Christians were also travelling to Israel at government subsidised rate for pilgrimages. The idea of restoration of relation at ambassadorial level was, thus not seen as something extra-ordinary by the Babangida regime. Part of the reason for this could be deciphered from Babangida's personality as he had previously claimed that posterity would forgive those who took wrong decisions but would certainly not pardon those who out of fear of failure refuse to act. He had also opined that his two heroes were Hannibal and Shaka the Zulu who were great warriors during their lifetime.[71]

The spirit of reconciliation was extended to African states such as Cameroon and Equatorial Guinea. For instance, despite incessant provocation by Cameroon which often invaded Nigerian towns across the boundary of the two countries, the Babangida regime refused to retaliate. This was notwithstanding the fact that the domestic public opinion favoured a retaliatory action.

The Nigerian government instead sought haven in diplomatic negotiation so as to calm taut nerves. In avoiding military confrontation with Cameroon, the Babangida regime was simply attempting not to factionalise the African continent. It also did not want external powers to intervene in Africa on the pretext of such confrontation. Again, the Nigerian civil war experience where the country's neighbours collaborated with the federal government to win the war of unity informed the need for

---

[71] N.I. Nwosu "The role of Domestic Politics in Nigeria's Foreign Policy," *Ilorin Journal of Sociology*, vol. 1, no 1, February 1994, p. 25.

dialogue.[72] Nigeria's peculiar boundary situation where it is surrounded only by French-speaking countries also informed the need for caution.

As well, in spite of provocation from Equatorial Guinea, Nigeria resisted retaliatory measures. Instead, the country showed its goodwill by not only attempting to broker peace with Equatorial Guinea through the exchange of visits by officials of the two states, but also by giving material assistance to the latter. Hence, Nigeria gave Equatorial Guinea ₦5 million loan to help the country purchase consumer goods. The repayment of this loan was spread over 10 years with an interest rate of 5 per cent Nigeria also built an international, school at the cost of ₦5 million in Equatorial Guinea as well as provided an agricultural package to that country. The Babangida administration had earlier in 1989 donated a naval patrol boat to Equatorial Guinea.[73] Nigeria also constructed a 52-bed polyclinic at ₦1.7 million in Malabo.[74]

Nigeria in the spirit of reconciliation also let off an Equatorial Guinea military attaché in the country who was caught with hard drugs. This followed the intervention of President Nguema Mbasogo of Equatorial Guinea who sent his son, Teodoro Mbasogo, to plead for the release of the military attaché.[75]

In tolerating Equatorial Guinea, the Babangida regime believed it was serving the interest of Africa, as the centre-piece of Nigeria's foreign policy. It also believed that the

---

[72] Olajide Aluko (ed.) *The Foreign policies of African Countries*, Hodder & Stoughton, 1977, p. 165.

[73] *Newswatch* (Lagos), 25 November 1991, p. 29.

[74] Ibid., p. 29.

[75] *Newswatch* (Lagos) 14 December 1992, p. 35.

strategic importance of Equatorial Guinea to both the Nigerian internal and external security would be well served by this. For instance, it is known that many Nigerian labourers who cannot be absorbed by the depressed economy of the country are working in Equatorial Guinea. Repatriating them home by their host state would have political, economic and security implications for Nigeria.

As part of efforts to reduce tension in the world, particularly in Africa, the Babangida regime intervened in several intra- and inter-state conflicts. Of particular reference was the government's mediatory role in the border dispute between Mali and Burkina Faso early in the life of the administration.[76] The Babangida's government also intervened to resolve the Chadian conflict. The intervention of the regime in this crisis stemmed from the involvement of extra Chadian forces particularly Libya and France, two countries that seemed to have special stake in the civil war. In fact, Bolaji Akinyemi, the Nigerian minister of external affairs contended that the presence of Libyan troops in Chad was bad and that the increased arms supply by France and the United States was inimical to the interest of Nigeria.[77]

It should be recalled that both the Shehu Shagari's government and Muhammadu Buhari regime had intervened to stop the Chadian dispute. That the Babangida regime still got the country involved in the resolution of the conflict perhaps illustrates the importance attached to peace in that country by the Nigerian foreign policy elite. Part of the reason for this, outside the attempt to stop the involvement of non-Chadian forces, was to avoid crisis

[76] *Newswatch* [Lagos] 13 January 1986, p. 31.
[77] *Newswatch* [Lagos] 26 January 1987, p. 29.

very near the Nigerian border. Again, the Nigerian governments saw the country as a sub-regional power within West Africa and felt that its human and material resources bestow on it the right to act as a trouble-shooter within the sub-region. The Babangida regime thus used all available opportunities to mediate in the Chadian conflict. To some extent, the regime succeeded. At least, it got to a point where Libya, France and Chad agreed to avoid military confrontation.[78] In fact, external involvement seemed to have stopped with the handing over of Aouzou strip by Libya to Chad following the ruling of the International Court of Justice (ICJ).

Again, the Babangida regime sent a delegation led by the minister of state for external affairs, Mamman Anka, to the leaders of Senegal and Mauritania when both countries engaged each other in military confrontation over a border problem. Following from this intervention, both states agreed to resolve the matter amicably.

It was in this same spirit that Nigeria intervened in Sudan to resolve the conflict between the government of that country and the Sudan Peoples Liberation Army [SPLA]. It should however, be stated that this intervention failed to resolve the dispute as the belligerent after some days of meeting in Nigeria refused to reach an agreement.[79] It must, nonetheless, be said that Nigeria in intervening in this conflict was practicalising one of her foreign policy objective: Africa as the centre-piece. That the meeting failed to produce a positive result does not remove the fact that an effort was made to de-escalate the crisis.

Nigeria's greatest attempt at resolving external dispute

---

[78] *Newswatch* [Lagos] 4 September 1986, p.25.
[79] *Newswatch* [Lagos] 8 June, 1992, p. 37.

during the Babangida regime was, however, evidenced in the country's intervention in the Liberian civil war. Nigeria intervened with some other West African states when it became clear that there was no real political authority in Liberia. This followed the invasion of Liberia by the Charles Taylor-led National Patriotic Front of Liberia [NPFL] which challenged the authority of President Samuel Doe's regime. In intervening in Liberia, Nigeria and the four other countries that constituted the West African peace monitoring force [ECOMOG] felt that the only way to restore peace to Liberia was to bring the combatants to the conference table so as to resolve their differences. Hence, apart from sending the ECOMOG to stop the bloodbath in Liberia, several peace conferences were organised under the auspices of the West African Economic Community [ECOWAS] in order to bring peace to Liberia.[80]

The peace initiatives, however, did not achieve much as the Liberian belligerent refused to respect some of the decisions reached in them. Again, Taylor, the leader of the NPFL distrusted Nigeria's mediation. This was because he felt that the Babangida regime intervened in Liberia merely to maintain Doe in power and stop him from occupying the presidential seat. In fact, this suspicion led Taylor and his forces to commit atrocities against Nigerian civilians in Liberia. Of particular reference is the killing of two Nigerian journalists, Krees Imodibie, the political editor of *The Guardian* and Tayo Awotusin of the *Champion* newspaper. Taylor's suspicion of Babangida's intention in Liberia should not be dismissed easily as the Nigerian president had prior to the crisis shown great admiration for Doe. This could be seen from his speech when he said 'the

---

[80]*The Guardian* [Lagos] 9 February, 1991, p. 9.

good thing about Doe is that he is the first indigenous local person to head Liberia since independence. And he makes sure these Liberians are very much in the affairs of the country. I respect him for that.'[81]

This notwithstanding, Nigeria and, indeed, the ECOWAS intervention in the Liberian conflict might have resulted from their concern for the Liberian and foreign civilian population who were trapped in the war zone. As Babangida stated:

> We are in Liberia because events in that country have "led to the massive destruction of property, the massacre by all the parties of thousands of innocent civilians including foreign nationals, women and children, some of whom sought sanctuary in churches, mosques, diplomatic missions, hospital and under the Red Cross protection, contrary to all recognised standard of civilised behaviour" and international ethics and decorum.[82]

The intervention by ECOMOG could also have resulted from the resolve to avoid extra African involvement in a purely African crisis. The desire to give a military dimension to the ECOWAS concept could also have necessitated the intervention. There was also the notion that Nigeria possesses superior military might that could be used to bring the warring groups to order. As Ahmed Fulani had argued, Nigeria's overall military power is superior to that of the fifteen countries within the West

---

[81] *Newswatch* [Lagos] 8 January, 1990, p. 20

[82] Tunji Olagunju & Sam Oyovbaire (eds.), *For their tomorrow, we gave our today,* Ibadan: Safari Books, 1991, p. 273.

African sub-region combined.[83]

Aside from the above, the Liberian imbroglio provided for Babangida another opportunity to demonstrate the resoluteness and decisiveness of his government. Nigeria's intervention in the Liberian conflict could, therefore, be seen as a projection of the decisiveness of his regime in matters affecting Africa. It was also believed that the experiences gained by the Nigerian soldiers in the ill fated Chadian peace keeping operation in the early 1980s could be valuable in the resolution of the Liberian conflict. That the conflict assumed even a bigger dimension including the occasional ECOMOG shooting with the warring factions showed clearly that Babangida's conflict resolution in Liberia failed to succeed. Indeed, the Nigerian leadership sensing that ECOMOG could not on its own resolve the conflict invited the United Nations [UN] to intervene. The UN has since stepped in to find solution to the six-year old war.

Apart from these instances, Nigeria under Babangida participated in finding armistice in war torn countries. These include participation in some of the several UN peace-keeping efforts such as the ones in Namibia, Rwanda, Somalia and Yugoslavia. In all these occasions, Nigeria showed her interest in world peace as either her soldiers or police men were highly commended for their level-headedness. In fact, a Nigerian, Ezidinma Ifejika was assigned the deputy leader of the United Nations Transition Assistance Group (UNTAG) Police Monitoring Unit during

---

[83] Ahmed S. Fulani, "Nigeria: Strategic Ambitions and West African Security," *Review of International Affairs*, vol. XL, no 950, 5 November 1989, p. 18.

the process of Namibia's independence.[84]

Decolonisation

Elimination of all shades of colonialism from the African region attracted the attention of the Babangida regime. The desire to liberate the continent was illustrated in the way the regime attended to the Namibian and South African independence questions. The Babangida regime used all available opportunities to call the attention of the world to the evils of colonialism and racism in Namibia and South Africa respectively. Apart from this, the government showed concrete support for the South West African Peoples Organisation (SWAPO) and the African National Congress (ANC), the two principal liberation movements in these countries by its moral and material supports to them. It was partly for this reason that Nigeria was invited as one of the first countries to establish diplomatic presence in Windhoek by the Namibian government following the country's independence in 1990.

Nigeria's resolve to ensure the liberation of Africa during this era was perhaps most noticeable in her role towards black majority rule in South Africa. This was seen in several respects. One of these was the Nigerian-led boycott of the 1986 Edinburgh Scotland Commonwealth Games. Nigeria led many countries to boycott this game due to the British government's intransigence over the question of black majority rule in South Africa. Again, the Babangida regime showed its resolve by its frequent attack on the apartheid South African government even at the time

---

[84] *Newswatch* (Lagos) 8 May, 1989, p. 23.

President Frederick W de Klerk regime had begun to show signs of change in its racist apartheid policy. This was done so as not to allow the white minority government to relax on the changes which were necessitated by local and external pressures. The way Nigeria under Babangida received the release of Nelson Mandela from the prison and his invitation to visit the country also showed the regime's anti-apartheid stance. This could also be seen in the award of an honorary doctorate degree by the University of Lagos to, and the conferment of the Grand Commander of the Order of the Niger on Mandela by Nigeria.[85] That Nigeria did not relax in her call for black majority rule even after this demonstrates the tenacity of purpose of the Babangida administration.

At this juncture, it must be stated that in as much as Nigeria's role in the enthronement of black majority rule in South Africa is commendable, the elimination of white minority rule in the country resulted mostly from the sustained resistance of the South African black population. This included intense guerrilla warfare, economic sabotage through strikes and physical destruction, and a vigorous and successful international campaign to ostracise the apartheid regime. Again, the changing international order following the collapse of Soviet Union convinced the South African government and her foreign supporters that the days of apartheid in world affairs were virtually over.

Projection of Nigerian and African Personality

Making the world to belief in the competence of Nigerian

---

and African people marked a significant signpost of Babangida's foreign policy. This perspective was shown early in the life of the regime when it allowed Rilwanu Lukman, Nigeria's oil minister, to take up the post of President of the Organisation of Petroleum Exporting Countries [OPEC]. Lukman not only performed this function creditably but also held the post for seven successive terms. Lukman's ability to steer the OPEC well led to the election of another Nigerian oil minister, Jubril Aminu, into the same post for four consecutive terms. Aminu's successor, Chu Okongwu, was also made an alternate OPEC president.

The resolve to show that Nigeria and, indeed, Africa had come of age encouraged the Babangida administration to sponsor Emeka Anyaoku as the secretary general of the Commonwealth. Joseph Garba, Nigeria's permanent representative at the UN was also sponsored as the president of the 44th Session of the UN General Assembly. That the two Nigerians won the elections indicates that the international community appreciates that Nigeria and Africa had capable people who can compete favourably with their peers all over the world.

The Babangida regime also sponsored its former attorney general and minister of justice, Bola Ajibola into the ICJ to replace Taslim Elias, the former president of the court who died in service. Bola Ajibola's victory in the election again manifested the trust which the international community has on Nigerian and African personality. That Ajibola after his tenure was appointed into the constitutional court of Bosnia by that country's government indicated an appreciation of his judicial pronouncements when he was in ICJ.[86]

These successes perhaps stimulated the Babangida regime into leading a campaign for an African secretary general of the UN. This was at the expiration of the term of office of Javier Perez De Cuellar who was the then incumbent. Arguing for an African UN secretary general, Babangida made it clear that Africa was not seeking for a favour from the world community, rather the continent was demanding for its due.[87] The Babangida regime did not stop at this. It sponsored a former Nigerian head of state, Olusegun Obasanjo, to contest for the post. This was an indication that the government meant what it was advocating. Eventually, six Africans contested for the position which was won by Boutros Ghali of Egypt. Ghali's victory owes much to Nigeria's insistence on an African Secretary General of the UN. This is so because, it was partly based on that demand that the international community became sensitised towards realising that Africa could produce capable candidates for such post. It also came partly as a result of the reconciliation efforts of Babangida.

In the same light, the Babangida regime following the evolving international order called for the democratisation of the UN Security Council. President Babangida's call centred essentially on the need for Africa, Asia and Latin America to be represented in the Security Council as permanent members. According to Babangida, the current arrangement where only Britain, China, France, Russia and the United States constitute the permanent membership does not represent the strength and the- universality of the

---

[86] *Sunday Times* (Lagos) 19 March, 1995, p. 11
[87] *Newswatch* [Lagos], 17 June 1991, p. 37.

UN.[88] Babangida posited that Africa with about one-third of the UN membership deserves at least a permanent seat in the Security Council. In making this demand, Babangida indicated that Nigeria is the most qualified African state to represent the continent as a permanent member of the Security Council. His reasons included country's population, which is the highest in the continent, and also the abundance of material and natural resources in Nigeria.

The call for an African permanent membership of the Security Council has gained momentum as many states have joined in the demand. Presently, there is a move towards the reformation of the Security Council in this light. It must, however, be noted that some other African countries have begun to question Nigeria's claim of being the most eligible state to represent the continent in the Security Council as a permanent member.

Economic and social justice

The depressed economy of Nigeria and indeed, Africa forced the Babangida regime to think of a way of bailing the continent out of this problem. One way envisioned by the regime was the demand for reparation against the long years of slavery and colonialism of the African continent. According to Babangida:

> We make these demands because the services of our fore-fathers in the American plantation were unrewarded and unpaid for. We make these

---

[88] Ibid., p. 36.

demands because the exploitation of Africa during
the period of colonial rule further impoverished us
and enhanced the development of the West.[89]

The quest for reparation was initiated by non-government persons and groups. One of the well-acknowledged initiator of reparation is Moshood Abiola. However, over time, the Babangida regime took over the cause for reparation and projected it to the level of the summit of the heads of state and government of the Organisation of African Unity [OAU]. Babangida's argument for reparation was so persuasive that the 26th assembly of heads of state and government of the OAU adopted it, and decided to set up an OAU Eminent Persons Group on Reparation.[90] The adoption of the reparation cause by the OAU indicates clearly that the African leaders believed that the achievement of this goal would help ginger up the continent's recessed economy. Currently, even some countries outside the African region have joined in the call for reparation.

Aside from this, the Babangida regime initiated and supported the African Economic Community [AEC]. According to Babangida, some of the advantages of a strong economically integrated region are the creation of bigger market for primary and finished products. it also includes reduction in the gap between the developing and the less developed states within the region.[91]

The charter of the AEC was adopted in Abuja in 1991. It is hoped that when the charter is fully operational, it would uplift the continent out of its dependent economic

[89] Olagunju & Oyovbaire, *loc. cit.*, p. 247.
[90] *Newswatch* [Lagos] 13 July, 1992, p. 32.
[91] *Newswatch* (Lagos) 10 February, 1992, p. 23.

relations with the developed economies. Nigeria's desire to create an African market for her products especially following the introduction of economic diplomacy must have informed the country's enthusiasm towards the formation of the AEC. It is, however, important to note that four years after the formation of the AEC, not much effort has been expended by African leaders towards its successful take off. Instead, most of the states in the continent including Nigeria have remained essentially dependent on the economies of Europe and America. Perhaps, this is mostly because the economies of most of these countries are underdeveloped and remain at the level of production of primary goods. The transformation of these into finished products largely depended not just on the raw materials from outside, but also on the technology of the advanced economies of the North.

It is perhaps to bridge this that the Nigerian government under Babangida introduced the technical aid corps scheme (TAC] to help needy African states and those in Diaspora.[92] The TAC scheme has to a large extent achieved its purpose as some of the corps members have been retained by their host countries at the expiration of their service. The Babangida administration was, however, not able to meet the demands of some countries on TAC scheme. This was because some of this manpower was not available in Nigeria and those present were already engaged.

Another area addressed by the Babangida regime was the question of external debt of developing countries. President Babangida continually harped on this because

---

[92] N.I. Nwosu "Foreign Policy in a Depressed Economy: The Nigerian Case Study," *The Government*, vol. 7, 1993, p. 33.

according to him 'prosperity like security is indivisible. The division of the world into a rich minority and a poor majority poses a threat to international peace and security.'[93]

In spite of this exhaustion, the debt profile and the rate of impoverishment of many developing countries have continued to increase. This indicates that the creditors are not interested in whatever reasons that are proffered for debt cancellation. In fact, Prime Minister Thatcher during one of her visits to Nigeria claimed that Nigeria is rich enough that the country does not deserve debt cancellation.[94]

Accommodation with global institutions and formation of international organisations

A noticeable practice in Nigeria's foreign policy under Babangida was the readiness to reach accommodation with global institutions. This attitude might have resulted from the belief of the administration that one way of reviving the depressed economy of Nigeria was through such accommodation. It was for this reason that one of the early actions of the Babangida regime was to resolve the impasse between Nigeria and the IMF over whether the country should accept or reject the latter's loan. That Babangida allowed the Nigerian public to participate in the debate over the IMF loan illustrates the decision of the regime not to antagonise the IMF if the loan is eventually rejected. And, it was rejected. It was again to prepare the Nigerian public

---

[93] *Newswatch* (Lagos] 17 June, 1991, p. 37
[94] *Newswatch* (Lagos] 10 April, 1989, p. 20.

to accept easily the consequences of such rejection. In rejecting the IMF loan, the Babangida regime ensured that it reached a compromise with the international financial institution by agreeing to implement most of its 'conditionalities'. Some of these include, trade liberalisation, removal of government subsidy, devaluation of the naira, privatisation and commercialisation. This compromise position by the Babangida regime helped the government to reach agreement with both the London and Paris clubs over debt rescheduling and negotiation. It thus, helped the regime to cushion the nation's economy to a certain degree.

It was perhaps based on the conviction that a well-integrated West African economy would be highly beneficial to Nigeria that the Babangida regime invested must in the ECOWAS. It is on record that the Babangida regime donated ₦5 million towards the building of the ECOWAS permanent headquarters in Abuja. This amount represents 33.33 % of the estimated ₦15 million budgeted for the building. Nigeria under Babangida provided 34 residential quarters to senior staff of ECOWAS.[95] All these were done in the hope that it would facilitate the performance of the secretariat-staff, which will in turn help the Nigerian and West African economies. This hope did not materialise, as several other Went African states did not show enough interest towards sub-regional economic integration. Instead, many of the West African countries saw the Babangida's gestures as attempts by Nigeria to control them.

Attempts to accommodate global institutions resulted in the various decisions by the Babangida regime to form

---

[95] *Newswatch* [Lagos] 14 July 1986, p. 26.

new international organisations. Hence, that regime played a big role in the formation of a group of five high crude producers within the OPEC.[96] It also participated actively in the formation of the African petroleum producers association [APPA] in Lagos in 1987.[97]

These organisations were formed mainly to assist the member countries derive the greatest benefit from the international oil market. It is, however, necessary to state that apart from the initial euphoria evident at the formation of these bodies, little was heard of them later.

Perhaps, the formation of the 'concert of medium powers' in 1986 by Nigeria represents the high point of the Babangida regime's zeal for the establishment of international organisations. According to Bolaji Akinyemi:

> The Lagos Forum defines a medium power in regional terms, and there can be no question that Nigeria is the pre-eminent military, economic and political power in sub-Saharan Africa. Nigeria is the largest African country...Nigeria's GDP is greater than that of all the other countries combined.[98]

This was in response to domestic and external criticisms over the formation of the 'concert of medium powers'. That the concert of medium powers did not survive beyond the ministerial tenure of Bolaji Akinyemi as external affairs minister, its acknowledged originator,

---

[96] *Newswatch* [Lagos] 16 December 1991, p. 29.

[97] Chibuzo N. Nwoke "Nigeria's Decision to Initiate the Formation of the African Petroleum Producers' Association" in Gabriel O. Olusanya & R. A. Akindele (eds.), *The Structure and Process of Foreign policy Making and Implementation in Nigeria 1960-1990*, Lagos: NIIA, 1990, pp. 479-487.

[98] *New Nigerian* [Kaduna] 8 May, 1987.

indicates the lack of planning and purpose in the formation of such international body. It also illustrates how the personality traits of Nigerian leaders have affected the country's foreign policy. Again, the collapse of the concert of medium powers shows that the machinery for the sustenance of such a body did not exist at its inception, and nobody cared to provide one.

Concluding comments

Nigeria's foreign policy under Babangida indicated the desire of the regime to use the country's external relations to ameliorate the depressed domestic economy. This was evidenced by the efforts of the regime to win the confidence and the sympathy of the international community. The Babangida regime, for instance, bent backwards to accommodate states such as Britain, the United States and Israel which it felt could help in leading Nigeria out of its predicament. It must, however, be stated that despite these attempts, these states, especially the first two did not reciprocate the way expected of them by the Babangida regime. They rather remained cautious in their dealings with Nigeria.

The regime's foreign policy also demonstrated several personality traits of the president and his foreign ministers. The IMF loan debate, crisis management in Africa and the formation of international institutions represent some of the foreign policy moves that reflected these personality traits. It also showed that the president and his foreign ministers were key players in the country's external relations.

The impact of the changing world order was also

noticed in Babangida's foreign policy. Evidence of this abounds in Nigeria's desire to participate actively in international institutions. It was also shown in the quest by the Nigerian foreign policy elite to help reshape the international system based on current events in the world. Hence, there was the call for more Nigerian and African active participation in international organisations as well as the democratisation of the UN Security Council.

In doing all these, the Babangida regime was mindful of its domestic economic problem. Opportunities offered by various international interactions were used to demand different forms of assistance to resuscitate the economy.

It should, therefore, be noted that Nigeria's foreign policy under the Babangida regime was partly built around the need to rejuvenate the national economy, as well as to project the country as an important member of the international community. This, the regime demonstrated in its foreign policy actions.

www.ingramcontent.com/pod-product-compliance
Lightning Source LLC
Chambersburg PA
CBHW021835020426
42334CB00014B/632